The Social Golf Course

Increasing Rounds with Social Media

By:
Zeb Welborn from 19th Hole Media
and
John Hakim from Greenskeeper.org

Contents

A Foreword by David Kramer

I had the opportunity to read an advance draft of "The Social Golf Course" while traveling with my son, Andrew, a professional golfer. We were headed to Orlando, Florida for the National Golf Course Owners Association, Superintendents of America and Club Manager's Association annual meeting. Los Serranos Country Club, my family-owned golf course built by my father, Jack Kramer, was one of four finalists for the National Golf Course of the Year.

From Orlando we drove to Pinehurst, North Carolina, the home of golf for North America, where the 2015 United States Open will be held for men and women. I had the privilege and the honor of playing Pinehurst No. 2 with Andrew.

Pinehurst reflects the spirit of the game, the traditions, the history, the inclusivity of the sport in the United States, in the same manner St. Andrews, the home of golf in Scotland, reflects them to the world.

The Social Golf Course was so compelling and intriguing that even the high-intensity turbulence encountered over the Rocky Mountains on the flight home to California wasn't enough to break my library-silenced concentration while reading this book by Zeb Welborn and John Hakim.

I know John Hakim from having met him one week after my father passed away in 2009 at the beautiful La Quinta Golf Resort in the Coachella Valley.

He was giving a speech to a group of successful golf course owners and operators about Greenskeeper. org. His message was strong and clear about the immense practical benefit golfers and golf course owners provide for one another.

It was another lucky day. I will never forget the gracious acknowledgment of my father's week-old passing.

I know Zeb Welborn.

I know his father, Larry, a recently retired legal affairs reporter for the Orange County Register. And, more importantly, a passionate historian and golf writer.

I know his mother, Ann, whose golf credentials include being the granddaughter of William Sime, a clubmaker at the Elie Golf Club in the late 1800s, located at the entrance to the Firth of Forth, west of Edinburgh.

I know his cousin, Ryan, who played in the 1999 U.S. Open Golf Championship at Pinehurst No. 2.

Therefore, I'm reasonably assured Zeb and John have a rich heritage that goes deep to the heart for the love of the game. And this is a good place to start a foreword to a book written by Zeb Welborn and John Hakim, both guardians and custodians, for owners and operators of golf facilities around the world who also love the game.

And I'm also certain owners and operators of businesses in other industries will find an inspiring introduction to the practical benefits social media can provide for improving your relationship building with your marketplace and patrons.

Zeb and John's skillful knowledge and expertise on quality communication content, coupled with their growing appreciation for the evolving range of social media technology make them a perfect match for any and every successful organization.

A successful organization is always searching for new and innovative solutions and remedies in an ever-changing and highly-competitive marketplace.

So, it was thus, a fortuitous merger when our family-owned and operated golf course invited Zeb to come and coach us. By introducing us to the powerful effects and multiple avenues of social media, our voice to our patrons and the marketplace has happily enriched our capacity for creating valuable relationships and keeping them.

Being exposed to the menu of possible social media opportunities delivered to us by 19th Hole Media and Greenskeeper.org was effectively encased in the core value all successful businesses strive to own.

And that core value lives in the heart of the Zeb and John I know. They love what they do and they cherish the knowledge they are sharing. As educators, they know the importance of getting to the heart of all that matters in the relationship between business owners and customers.

Zeb and John know that to be successful, communication must be authentic and thorough. The story of a business must be communicated with a powerful emotional resonance that can be shared from one heart to another. Love.

This is the building block of wisdom that will create an initial condition that will trigger business outcomes that can't be anticipated. This is real, life-force leverage that comes from being true to yourself. Zeb and John's willingness and generosity to share their knowledge and enthusiastic aim to support the interest of their clients will make for an inevitable mutually-enriching relationship.

Therefore, as you witness the growth of your company's capacity to create inspiring and competent dialogue with your current customers and future customers, it is guaranteed that you too will know the knowledge and expertise that relevant social media will provide to your organization.

Lastly, even if Zeb Welborn and John Hakim are strangers to you, I can attest that their family-style approach will immediately and rigorously charm and move you to be part of this family.

If it is possible to state an endorsement for Zeb and John's vision of your social media relationship with your company, then it can be made based on the championship results our family business has experienced.

I'd be happy to further elaborate this foreword on the soothing, and captivating words that I so enjoyed reading even during a rough and tumble turbulence effect on a transcontinental flight over the Rocky Mountains. I can continue this foreword gladly at (909) 815 - 7184.

INTRODUCTION

Tee It High and Let It Fly: Time to Embrace Social Media

Social media is changing our economy ... forever.

Offline and online worlds have collided. They will forever be intertwined. To stay competitive, golf courses must build authentic relationships that translate into business.

These relationships must help trigger the most effective form of advertising -- word of mouth -- taking place on social platforms in exponentially growing numbers.

We've talked with golf course owners, general managers and directors of golf across the United States.

The sentiment is usually the same:

"I don't understand social media," one general manager said.

"Social media is a fun thing to do, but it doesn't benefit our golf course in a substantial way," said a director of golf.

"We're doing social media, but it's not working," a golf course marketing director said.

If you find yourself with similar doubts, concerns or worries, you should read this book: social media works.

Here's what the Director of Golf at Arroyo Trabuco Golf Club -- 19th Hole Media's client for six months -- said: "We wanted to thank our customers on our Facebook page, by offering discounted rounds, but we can't because we're booked solid until 4pm."

The General Manager at San Dimas Canyon Golf Course -- 19th Hole Media's client for eight months -- said: "We've had the best month we've ever had at this time of the year, and in comparison with other golf courses similar to ours . . . we're doing extremely well."

And as Tom Robinson, a golfer at Los Serranos Country Club, said: "Its been a year since adding Los Serranos to my "likes" list (on Facebook) and in that time I've played five rounds (never as a single) at the country club. Traditionally I will play maybe two total rounds per year at the course because of where I live."

Many golf course owners and operators are failing to see the potential of social media. And the potential is massive.

We can't ignore change and change is upon us all. People are consuming information at an unprecedented rate. And the best way to be heard in the noise of information bombarding golfers is to reach them relevantly: as they are deciding when and where to play.

And that is happening on social media -- effective social media.

Social media can help your golf course communicate with golfers 24 hours a day, seven days a week. Imagine having thousands of golfers talking about your golf course daily when they aren't even at your course. And the best part is the value you create -- is yours.

You get the benefit, not golf magazines or tee time wholesalers. By using social media effectively, you are communicating directly to the golfer and future customer rather than through a third party, achieving brand loyalty.

So, the culture of a golf course should change to incorporate the social media online world into the traditional offline world to create the 21st century golf course -- The Social Golf Course.

Throughout the book, we've included opportunities for you to engage with us. At the end of every chapter we pose a question. We encourage you to engage, interact and share your ideas with us at SocialGolfCourse. com

"Alone we can do so little; together we can do so much." - Helen Keller

CHAPTER 1

The Death of the Traditional Golf Course

"The 1960s were an exceptionally vibrant time in history and in golf. Upward of six million people were playing the game in the United States at the start of the decade, generating a billion dollars a year." — Howard Sounes[1]

When I think of the glory days of golf, I imagine the time period following World War II. Veterans returned victorious from war and the economy was booming. Families across the country were creating the middle class and participating in recreational activities ... perhaps the biggest being golf.

My grandfather, John Welborn, was the President of the Men's Club at Western Hills Country Club; one of the most prestigious titles any community member could have. I think back to what it must have been like at the clubhouse on a busy Saturday afternoon. Hus-

---

1 Sounes, Howard. The Wicked Game: Arnold Palmer, Jack Nicklaus, Tiger Woods, and the Story of Modern Golf. New York: W. Morrow, 2004. Print.

bands, wives and families visited their local golf courses regularly to be near the center of their community.

Businessmen conducted their business on the golf course. They took the four hour round to get to know one another to decide if they wanted to do business with each other.

Political leaders often frequented the golf course, many establishing leadership roles as a result of their involvement with the Men's Club or the golf course.

And local economies benefited with the success of their local golf course.

The local golf course was the social, political and economic hub of many communities in America.

In my vision of the traditional golf course, I imagine a bustling clubhouse raging with activity. Community members, business leaders and politicians interacting with one another on a regular basis. At one table is a group of two twosomes who were paired together on the golf course and are now interacting with one another as if they've known each other their entire lives. At another table is a foursome who have played with each other every weekend for the past decade. At another table, a business conversation is taking place and agreements are made to build and grow two local businesses. At another table, politicians are discussing ideas for new policies to implement, and at yet another table is a group of frequent, loyal visitors to the golf course who come regularly because they enjoy the hustle and bustle of the clubhouse.

But to quote Bob Dylan, "The times they are a-changin."

This vision of the bustling clubhouse as envisioned above will not, and can not exist in our new economy. Business conversations, political conversations and social conversations are taking place in different locations than they were 60 years ago.

As an industry, we need to accept these changes and work with them to replicate an environment as it was in the years following World War II. A vibrant, active community where community leaders and members interact and engage with one another to help build a better, stronger community.

Local golf courses are no longer the social, political and economic hub of their communities. But . . . it's not because they shouldn't be, it's because many golf courses have given up the role.

Social, political and business conversations are happening every day online. People are consuming, absorbing and sharing information at an unprecedented rate and they are looking for organizations which can attract and bring like-minded individuals together. Most local golf courses failed to capitalize on this shift in our economy and the industry as a whole has suffered.

Our mission with this book is to make the golf course a social, political and economic hub of local communities once again.

We're here to modernize our idealized version of the traditional golf course and usher in a new era . . . the era of the social golf course.

Discuss at SocialGolfCourse.com
When were the glory days of golf?

CHAPTER 2

An Industry in the Rough

*"The game was technically open to all, and the
St Andrews links, like most links, occupied
public land. But few workingmen could afford
to play in an age when whole families, including
both parents as well as children as young as
five or six, toiled six days a week to earn what
a gentleman spent to buy a single golf ball."* —
Kevin Cook[2]

John attended the Crittenden Golf Conference
in Phoenix in October, 2013. At the conference they
spelled out the current state of the golf course industry.

Since 2000, the United States golf course industry
has lost 123 million rounds per year. During the same
time period, we have added 2,000 new golf courses. The
supply of golf courses increased substantially while the
demand for golf decreased substantially as well.

---

2 Cook, Kevin. Tommy's Honor: The Story of Old Tom Morris and Young Tom
Morris, Golf's Founding Father and Son. New York: Gotham, 2007. Print.

To indicate how bad it is, in 2011, 157 golf courses closed. In 2012, 155 more shut down. Nine out of 10 golf courses lost money in 2012. Participation of the general population in the sport was down from 12.9% in 2000 to 9% in 2011.

From 2005 to 2011, the number of golfers dropped from 30 million to 26 million. Core golfers declined from 18 million to 14.4 million. Not only that, but, in 2005 the "core golfer" was defined as someone who played 24 rounds per year. In 2011, the definition of a "core golfer" was someone who played eight rounds per year.

In 2011, 3.5 million golfers took up the game. But during the same year we lost 3.9 million golfers. In 2011, we had a net loss of 400,000 golfers.[3]

We should note that while our industry overall has been struggling since 2005, there are some positive signs. As the economy continues its turnaround, so has golf.

In 2012, 500 million rounds were played, a 5.7% increase in rounds played from 2011.[4]

In an article featured on the Bloomberg website, According to Golf, the Economy is Out of the Rough, the National Golf Foundation expects the number of golfers to grow by about three million between 2010 and 2020.

And in 2012, 500 million rounds were played, a 5.7% increase in rounds played from 2011.[5]

Social media has helped and can continue to help this promising trend climb faster.

---

3 Session 101: Opening Keynote - State of the Golf Industry." Proc. of Crittenden Golf Conference, Phoenix. N.p.: n.p., n.d. N. pag. Print.

4 "According to Golf, the Economy Is Out of the Rough." Bloomberg.com. Bloomberg, n.d. Web. 12 Feb. 2014.

5 "According to Golf, the Economy Is Out of the Rough." Bloomberg.com. Bloomberg, n.d. Web. 12 Feb. 2014.

The Blame Game: The Golf Course Industry Response to Declines

The response from the golf course industry has lacked innovation. They have focused on blaming external factors and/or customers rather than taking responsibility for their inability to connect with today's golfers.

At the same Crittenden Golf Conference, industry leaders shared reasons why they thought the golf course industry was falling behind.

- People Have Less Time
- More Family Oriented Free Time
- Difficult Game to Learn and Get Good At
- Younger Generation Wants Instant Results
- More Women and Minority Participation Needed
- Cost Factor: Expensive to Play - Equipment, "Proper Clothes"
- Intimidation Factor
- Difficult Courses, It Should Be Fun Not Torture [6]

As the Director of Golf at El Prado Golf Course said in a discussion he had with Zeb, "They are blaming others."

The golf course industry is placing the blame for their declines on external factors instead of creating solutions.

None of the reasons listed take accountability for the lack of growth in the game in recent years. They do not offer constructive solutions to problems. These identi-

---

6 "Session 101: Opening Keynote - State of the Golf Industry." Proc. of Crittenden Golf Conference, Phoenix. N.p.: n.p., n.d. N. pag. Print.

fying issues are nothing new. Many are exaggerated. Some are inaccurate. Let us tell you why.

Do People Have Less Free Time?

According to the Bureau of Labor Statistics we now have more free time and work fewer hours than our parents. In 1964, the average work week was over 38 hours. In 2013, the average work week is under 34 hours.[7]

Is More Family-Oriented Free Time Hurting Golf Courses?

Golf is a social game which gives people of all skills and abilities the chance to head out on the golf course. How can this be detrimental to the golf course industry?

Is Golf a Difficult Game to Learn and Get Good At?

Golf is a difficult game to learn and get good at . . . and it has always been. To say people are not playing golf now because it's too difficult is ridiculous. It has always been a hard game.

Does the Younger Generation Want Instant Results?

Generalizing the younger generation in this way can be damaging to the golf course industry. While some may demand instant results, others will understand that hard work, commitment and dedication will deliver results.

---

7 Hargreaves, Steve. "Why We're Working Less than Our Parents Did." CN-NMoney. Cable News Network, 29 July 2013. Web. 12 Feb. 2014.

Our feeling is the younger generation is just as apt to play the game as the generation before them. But, we must make it enjoyable. Social media can bring golfers together, and provide young golfers with a more compelling reason to play.

Every generation has a tendency of blaming their younger counterparts and, usually, the blame is misplaced.

Do We Need More Women and Minority Participation in Golf?

Yes, absolutely. We should work to get as many golfers, of all backgrounds, playing golf.

Is Golf Too Expensive?

The price of golf has not substantially risen or fallen. The cost factor is nothing new. In fact, in the keynote at the 2013 October Crittenden Golf Conference, the average green fee was quoted at $28.[8]

Are People Too Intimidated to Play Golf?

Sure, some people are intimidated and don't pick up the game because of that, but again, this has always been the case.

Are Golf Courses Too Difficult?

Some golfers may get frustrated because of the difficulty of a golf course. Using social media as a listening tool can help us understand the frustrations golfers are

---

8 "Session 101: Opening Keynote - State of the Golf Industry." Proc. of Crittenden Golf Conference, Phoenix. N.p.: n.p., n.d. N. pag. Print.

experiencing and allow us to create solutions to make their experience more enjoyable.

We feel the golf course industry needs to take ownership of the decline of golf and focus on innovative ways to bring more golfers into the game.

Reasons Why Golf Numbers are Down

Our list would look something like this:

- Not effectively marketing the lifestyle benefits golf provides
- Not effectively marketing to families
- Not educating golfers on necessary skills to grow and learn
- Not introducing enough younger golfers to the game
- Not appealing to enough women and minorities
- Not creating enough opportunities to introduce lower socioeconomic classes to the game.
- Not performing enough outreach to entice "intimidated" would-be golfers to play
- Not setting up golf courses in a manner conducive to learning and enjoyment

The language we choose when identifying problems is extremely important. In the example we've given, we're taking responsibility and thinking of changes we can make to get more golfers playing more golf.

We need to change our mindset.

How Can We Effectively Market the Lifestyle Benefits Golf Provides?

Golf teaches valuable life lessons, is healthy and promotes social engagement. Local golf courses need to be active in demonstrating the lifestyle benefits golf can bring to the members of their community.

How Can We Market Better to Families?

Golf is a social game and -- according to the presentation at the Crittenden Golf Conference -- families are spending more quality time with each other. This should be great news for golf courses.

Los Serranos Country Club had an extremely successful family fun program. An adult and child could play for $20 with a cart whenever the tee was open. The program brought parents and children together, made golf a conversation at the family dinner table and generated additional revenue for the golf course.

By sharing, promoting and engaging with golfers about this program through social media, the impact would be even greater for golf, the golf course and the family.

How Can We Educate Golfers on Necessary Skills to Grow the Game?

Local golf courses can use social media to educate potential golfers before they ever step foot on the course.

Imagine creating a series of YouTube videos explaining etiquette, the proper swing and the local rules at your course. Potential golfers can become acquainted with the traditions of golf, local rules and learn the fundamentals of a golf swing from local golf professionals. They will view your course as one willing to educate, teach and grow beginning golfers.

Instead of being a source of intimidation, your golf course can open up opportunities for new players.

How Can We Introduce More Young Golfers to the Game?

Social media is constantly evolving and the earliest adopters are the younger generation. By creating a youth program and encouraging young golfers to share their golfing experiences through social media outlets, you are creating a tremendous word of mouth opportunity amongst the younger population.

To get younger golfers to play golf, we need to be able to speak their language. In today's world, their language is social media.

How Can We Appeal to More Women and Minorities?

A lot of females and minorities have never stepped foot on a golf course because they assume golf is a male dominant sport. By sharing photos, pictures and videos of females and minorities at your golf course on social media, you demonstrate that your golf course is one who welcomes women and minorities.

How Do We Get Lower Socioeconomic Classes to Participate in the Game?

Creating programs that will help introduce lower socioeconomic classes to golf and your golf course can have a substantial impact.

We often encourage golf courses to provide charitable work for their community. In our socially-driven world, charitable work provides a valuable service to the community. These services also create a valuable word of mouth opportunity to be shared on your social media outlets.

How Do We Make Golf Less Intimidating?

Social media posts create opportunities for those intimidated by golf to be exposed to the game. Golfers can be exposed to golf protocol, can be introduced to other golfers and have discussions with regular golfers. Intimidated golfers can ask questions of other golfers before they feel comfortable to jump out on the course and start to play.

Some, like Chris Pennington from Greenskeeper. org, said she took up the game because of her experience with golf on social media.

How Can We Set Up Golf Courses in a Manner Conducive to Learning and Enjoyment?

The best way to create an environment centered on enjoyment and learning is to use customer feedback to give your customers what they want. Social media is a tremendous listening tool we can use to learn what our customers think of our golf course and can adjust accordingly. Social media offers real-time, authentic feedback taking all the guess work out of setting up your golf course to make it more enjoyable and fun.

Summary:

By focusing on the things we can control, we can create a proactive environment where we strive for solutions instead of placing blame. By creating solutions we are making a difference. In the long run our efforts will be invaluable for the game.

Discuss at SocialGolfCourse.com

What is the biggest problem facing golf today? How can we fix it?

CHAPTER 3

The St. Andrews Model

"Every individual who has made a living out of hitting a golf ball should hold April 20th 1851 as the nativity for that was the birth date of Young Tom Morris, one of the game's greatest early exponents." [9]

It's been people with vision who have been instrumental in developing the game of golf. Luminaries such as Old Tom Morris, Young Tom Morris, Harry Vardon, James Braid, Bobby Jones, Walter Hagan, Ben Hogan, Arnold Palmer, Jack Nicklaus, Tiger Woods, and organizations such as the R&A and the PGA have had roles in supporting and promoting the game -- making golf what it is today.

Effective marketing has always been important.

Golf courses that appreciate the value and importance of effective marketing are the ones that left a lasting impact. Take St. Andrews, for example, which,

---

9 "History of Golf - Scottish Perspective." History of Golf - Scottish Perspective. N.p., n.d. Web. 16 Nov. 2013.

through effective marketing, became known as the home of golf.

How many know the first 11 Open Championships were played at Prestwick and not at St. Andrews?

> *"It was in 1860 that the first Open Championship was held at Prestwick and was contested by eight leading professionals. The first winner was Willie Park ... The Open continued to be held at Prestwick for 11 years and the Morris's dominated the early events. Old Tom had won the event four times by 1867 and Young Tom subsequently completed a quartet of wins, after which he was allowed to keep the Belt."* [10]

When the average golfer thinks of the origins of golf, he thinks of St. Andrews. But competitive golf started in Prestwick.

So, why do we think of St. Andrews as the "home of golf" and not Prestwick? Why is the Royal & Ancient, their local golf club, the body that oversees the golfing world? Why is playing the Old Course on every golfer's bucket list?

The answer -- marketing.

---

10 "History of Golf - Scottish Perspective." History of Golf - Scottish Perspective. N.p., n.d. Web. 16 Nov. 2013.

"The Open Championship has not been held at Prestwick since 1925. The Prestwick links doubled in size after the club bought land north of the old stone wall and extended the course from twelve to eighteen holes - the St. Andrews standard - but in time the tournament outgrew its birthplace. Today Prestwick is quiet, the breeze off the Firth of Clyde skimming shaggy dunes where the schoolboy Tom Morris ran. Goosedubs swamp is long gone, drained and re-turfed. The links' humps and hollows, blessedly free of whins in the Morrises' day, are chockablock with whins planted later to make the course look more like a "classic" links, which is to say more like St. Andrews. The only sign that the Open began here at Prestwick is a cairn on the spot where the first teeing-ground used to be. A plaque on the cairn gives the length of Tom's opening hole, 578 yards, and the date of the first Open, October 17, 1860. There is no mention of Tommy's miracle three on this hole in the 1870 Open, or his 1869 ace at the Station Hole, golf's first recorded hole-in-one, or his four consecutive Open victories on this course.

*St. Andrews is a different story. The town's
golf heritage is all over the place, from Tommy's
memorial in the Cathedral cemetery to the L90
hickory putters in the souvenir shop by the Home
green to the L822-a-nigh Royal & Ancient Suite
at the hulking Old Course Hotel to the golf-ball-
shaped mints in the Tourist Centre on Market
Street. This is Provost Playfair's dream come
true with a vengeance, the thousand-year-old
town reborn as golf's capital. Where generations
of religious pilgrims once came looking for Saint
Andrew's kneecap, golfers now make pilgrimages
to the Old Course. It was not the first course,
but it is the most important, due largely to the
work Tom Morris began here in 1864, when he
brought his family home from Prestwick."* [11]

The people at St. Andrews are responsible for that
reputation. They took it upon themselves to grow, foster and cultivate the game we all love . . . and they did
it at the local golf course level.

Prestwick faded away.

You can choose to be like Prestwick: not reach younger golfers, not grow the game and not market effectively.

Or, you can choose to be like St. Andrews: to innovate, to be social, to get people connected and to effectively market your golf course.

Make your model more like St. Andrews, the undis-
puted "home of golf."

---

11   Cook, Kevin. Tommy's Honor: The Story of Old Tom Morris and Young
Tom Morris, Golf's Founding Father and Son. New York: Gotham, 2007. Print.

Discuss at SocialGolfCourse.com

What are some interesting ways you've seen golf courses market themselves? How do/would you market your golf course?

CHAPTER 4

A Mulligan

"A U.S. citizen is vacationing on his own in Ireland. He decides to play a round of golf and is paired with three local gents. He takes a few practice swings, steps up to the first tee, and proceeds to hook the ball out of bounds. He shakes his head, reaches in his pocket, and re-tees another ball. He tells his playing partners that he is taking a Mulligan. He pounds one down the center of the fairway about 280 yards out.

With a big smile, he asks the others 'In the U.S., we call that a Mulligan; was wondering what you called it here in Ireland.'

After a moment of silence, one of the locals replies, 'Hitting three.'" — Cathy McCartney Happel [12]

---

12   "A Quick Nine: Best Golf Jokes." PGA.com. N.p., n.d. Web. 15 Feb. 2014.

In the early 2000s, golfers moved online to determine where to play and book tee times. At the time, golf courses were slow to react. They should have launched their own websites to cater to their golfers. Instead, golf courses moved like molasses while tee time wholesalers seized the opportunity to build their own network of golfers.

Wholesalers like Click4TeeTimes and GolfNow built websites attracting golfers looking for the best deal. Golfers signed up, handing over their email addresses. The wholesalers built their own database of golfers and used email marketing to attract a golf crowd who became loyal -- not to the local golf course -- but to the tee time wholesalers.

Shanked that one.

Now the golf course industry finds itself in a dependency model with tee time wholesalers where golf courses continue to give their customer relationships away and weaken their rate integrity.

Had the golf course industry been proactive in building websites, creating transaction portals and accumulating email addresses offering their own discounts and values, they would have developed a loyal customer base building an online/offline relationship with their customers.

Instead, they gave their relationships away. Now most golf courses need to slash prices to stay competitive.

But social media provides a mulligan.

In the 2010s, the golf industry is entering a new era of online marketing where they can win back customers and rebuild loyalty lost to the wholesalers in the 2000s.

Discuss at SocialGolfCourse.com
Are tee time wholesalers good or bad for the golf industry?

CHAPTER 5

Golf is a Social Game

"If you play golf, you are my friend." — Harvey
Penick [13]

Fred Shoemaker is a golf professional who taught
the game for 30 years, giving more than 42,000 lessons. In his book, Extraordinary Golf: The Art of the
Possible, he imagines writing himself a letter at the end
of his golfing career.

In the letter, Fred expresses resentment that he
didn't take advantage of all golf had to offer.

He goes on to say:

13   Wood, David. Around the World in 80 Rounds: Chasing a Golf Ball from
Tierra Del Fuego to the Land of the Midnight Sun. New York: St. Martin's, 2008.
Print.

"I wish I could have been a better playing partner . . . I wish I had been friendlier and gotten to know people better. I wish I could have laughed and joked more, and given people more encouragement. I probably would have gotten more from them, and I would have loved that . . . most of the people I played with were friendly, polite and sincere. They really just wanted to make friends and have a good time. I wish I could have made more friends and had a better time . . .

Play a game that gives you joy and satisfaction and makes you a better person to your family and friends. Play with enthusiasm, play with freedom. Appreciate the beauty of nature and the people around you. Realize how lucky you are to be able to do it. All too soon your time will be up, and you won't be able to play anymore. Play a game that enriches your life . . ."[14]

Imagine your customers writing a similar letter when they no longer play. I'll bet their response will not be proper mechanics, a smooth swing or a nice putting stroke. I'll bet they want to look back on their golfing career as one spent interacting with others while enjoying the great outdoors.

Because ... golf is social.

Give loyal golfers a platform -- through social media channels -- to talk about your golf course, to share

---

14 Shoemaker, Fred, and Pete Shoemaker. Extraordinary Golf: The Art of the Possible. New York: G.P. Putnam's Sons, 1996. Print.

experiences, and start dialogues, and they will be more receptive to your messages and your brand.

As David Kramer once said to me, "Golf was the first form of social media."

Golf, above all other sports, should be paving the way socially.

Discuss at SocialGolfCourse.com

What makes golf special?

CHAPTER 6

Marketing in Today's Economy

"I have no idea what the original intent was of the Scottish shepherds who presumably invented golf. Probably to while away some pretty boring hours in the fields. But it doesn't really matter, since we have the freedom to play the game for whatever reasons we choose . . . The purpose of golf . . . is for you to decide." [15] — Fred Shoemaker

Social media is young. Facebook has been around for only 10 years and other social media platforms far less. Yet the majority of Internet usage takes place on social media. In fact one out of every five internet page views in the United States is on Facebook. [16]

We are at the dawn of a cultural shift where the mergence of the physical world and cyberspace is moving at

---

15 Shoemaker, Fred, and Pete Shoemaker. Extraordinary Golf: The Art of the Possible. New York: G.P. Putnam's Sons, 1996. Print.

16 "Hitwise: Facebook.com Now Accounts For 1 In Every 5 Pageviews On The Web (In The U.S.)." TechCrunch. N.p., n.d. Web. 15 Feb. 2014.

a breathtaking pace. Hundreds of millions of dollars, every month, are invested in tech startups.

Anyone still doing something that worked five years, one year or even six months ago -- and hasn't changed -- is falling behind their competition.

Prior to the age of mass media (newspapers, magazines, radios and television), the power in the relationship between a business and the customer was with the customer. Think of the local woodworker or blacksmith. If they wanted to keep their business, they relied on word of mouth -- from their satisfied customers. This is the way most business was done until the creation of mass media ... when customers lost their voice.

From Mass Media to Social Media

The 20th Century can be marked by the rise of mass media. Newspaper, radio and television advertising brought information to the masses like never before.

But, it was an anomaly.

For far too long, consumers were dependent upon mass media to get new ideas, gather information and make purchasing decisions. People had access to information, but it was controlled by large corporations and the marketing methods with which they sold their products. Those who could afford marketing and advertising thrived.

However; marketing was inefficient, unwanted and left the power in the hands of the organizations who supplied the message. The customer was not in control.

Your Customer Now Has a Voice

In today's social age, the customer has a voice.

Businesses, organizations and individuals (the customers) can now publish content, share opinions, create an audience and thrive.

In 2010, Eric Schmidt, CEO of Google, said, "Every two days now we create as much information as we did from the dawn of civilization up until 2003." [17]

Customers can leave reviews, share experiences, generate ideas, foster discussions, share photos and videos. They are active. They are social.

And this...is a great thing for business.

In our new economy, the power lies in the consumers and the dynamic is shifting every day. Consumers choose the businesses they want to be associated with and avoid the messages they no longer want. They never wanted to be told what to buy ... they always wanted to choose for themselves.

The consumer can now determine which companies succeed and which will not. The companies that thrive in our new economy will use social cues and tools to alter their businesses to address the needs and desires of their customers.

Marketing: Push vs. Pull

On a daily basis we come face to face with messages from mass media. Most messages are "push" messages, meaning they interrupt us in our day and force us to stop and take notice. To put it mildly, they are annoyances.

Imagining a typical day we encounter these annoyances regularly:

---

17 "Eric Schmidt: Every 2 Days We Create As Much Information As We Did Up To 2003." TechCrunch. N.p., n.d. Web. 19 Nov. 2013.

I get home from work at around 5 p.m. and head straight to my mailbox. My mailbox is cluttered with unwanted coupons, flyers and advertisements. They immediately find their way to the recycle bin. Never to be looked at again.

To relax, I head inside to watch highlights from a golf tournament.. After a minute or two, a commercial airs . . . It's louder than the show and interrupts my enjoyment. Fortunately, I recorded the show on my DVR so I can skip through the unwanted interruption.

Later, I head to the kitchen to work with my wife to make our family dinner when the phone rings. I answer, "Hello, this is Zeb Welborn. How can I help you?"

There is a pause on the other line . . . a few seconds go by and the pre-taped recording on the other end begins . . . "Hi, my name is So and So and I work for So and So Business calling you about an exciting new opportunity . . ." The recorded message continues. I hang up, frustrated, lamenting the fact that So and So called me from So and So Company. I think to myself I will never use their services.

I head to my computer to check emails and see message after message from people I don't know and have never met selling who knows what. The messages do not relate to me. I figure out how to unsubscribe from their email lists.

How do you feel about the company that interrupted your day to send you those messages? Do you want your customers feeling the same way about you?

Those are all examples of "push" marketing. For businesses, some "push" marketing is necessary, but it needs to be done in an acceptable manner to uphold the reputation of the business.

Let's compare the "push" marketing day with a "pull" marketing campaign.

I get home from work at around 5pm and head straight for the mailbox. A personalized letter has been sent to me by my local golf course, thanking me for playing in their latest golf tournament. A nice message inside shares some personal insight into my relationship with the golf course. I smile.

To relax, I head inside to watch some YouTube videos online about the golf tournament. At the end of each video, YouTube offers me suggestions on other videos, which I watch continuously clicking from video to video, some are about golf products and services, others are just fun to watch.

Later, I head to the kitchen to work with my wife to make our family dinner when the phone rings. I answer, "Hello, this is Zeb Welborn. How can I help you?"

"Hi, my name is So and So and I work for So and So Golf Course calling you about the comment card you filled out when you visited our golf course. We wanted to thank you about the kind words you had to say about your last outing and for playing golf at So and So Golf Course." I hang up, thinking, "Wow."

I head to my computer to check my daily emails and see an email from So and So Golf Course, thanking me for signing up for their mailing list. I think back and remember seeing a signup form on the counter for their email newsletter offering discounts and contests for free golf. I signed up. I open the email to see discounts for the week of golf and I think to myself . . . "I will have to play golf at So and So golf course again."

We understand these are hypothetical scenarios, but we want you to understand the difference between "push" and "pull" marketing.

The advantage of "pull" marketing lies in your ability to reach out to the customers who really want your product or service.

The golf courses who figure out ways to incorporate "pull" marketing into their organizations will be the golf courses who succeed. If we get enough golf courses to work on figuring out "pull" marketing methods we can change the direction of the golf industry from a downward spiral to a force to be reckoned with.

Our Internal Filter: Avoiding Sales Messages

So, consumers want to control the message they receive. And social media makes it easier to target customers more specifically and personalize messages to individual consumers.

Our customers have the ability to control their own messaging, what companies they want to follow, which ones they choose to "like" and which ones they choose to ignore. But most importantly, they get to decide.

On a daily basis we're learning to filter out advertising messages we don't want. Zeb never watches live TV anymore because he can record the show on his DVR and fast forward through the commercials. He can tell instantly when he receives an email whether it's a genuine email or a sales message. He does not go out of his way to see sales messages because they do not add anything to his life.

They provide no value to him.

Those companies and golf courses that understand marketing is no longer about pushing out a sales message, but about creating conversations and connecting with individuals will pierce through the noise and help to bring more golfers into their niche. If you're pushing out sales messages you're losing. If you're authentically connecting, you're on your way to success.

Localizing Our Economy

Another change to our economy has been localization. Local businesses and organizations have a stronger ability to reach their customers through the internet, social media, search engine optimization and pay-per-click campaigns like Google AdWords.

As the internet grows and evolves, we foresee more and more importance placed on localizing results based off of your family, friends and contacts.

In January 2013, Google debuted 'Search Plus Your World' updating their popular search engine, giving preference to users logged into their Google+ accounts by including social content in their search results. By adding personalized results -- like showing who is in

your circle of contacts -- SPYW claims they revolution-
ized the search landscape. [18]

Meaning your search engine rankings are enhanced
by who you're connected to on social media.

For local golf courses, it means they will be responsible for promoting themselves online. The more people connected to your golf course online, the more likely
your golf course will show up in search engine results.

Cut Expenditures or Grow the Game?

The theme for many golf courses in recent years has
been to cut expenditures. Golf courses need to become
wiser with their money and spend it where it has the
most impact. Social media marketing can be more targeted, reach more people, reach people more frequently
and enhance word of mouth marketing more so than old
school marketing.

To grow the game, we should focus efforts at the local level using tools that give the most value for our
dollar; social media is the answer.

Discuss at SocialGolfCourse.com

**What is the future of marketing in the golf course
industry?**

---

18   "Google Plus Means SEO for Marketers." Search Engine Studio Search-
EngineStudio.com. N.p., n.d. Web. 04 Jan. 2014.

CHAPTER 7

The Golf Niche

"A golfer who got bad advice from his caddie, or detected laziness or cheek in him, was within his rights to backhand the caddie full in the face, or take a club and whip him with it." — Kevin Cook [19]

What is a Niche?

A niche is a position or activity that particularly suits somebody's talents and personality or that somebody can make his or her own.

The future of business will reside in niches and how large you're able to make yours. Today, people have unlimited access to information. They connect with others who have the same likes and dislikes, creating opportunities for growth -- socially and economically.

In 2010, Zeb started The Tutoring Solution, an inhome tutoring business in Southern California and he

---

19   Cook, Kevin. Tommy's Honor: The Story of Old Tom Morris and Young Tom Morris, Golf's Founding Father and Son. New York: Gotham, 2007. Print.

took to the internet to promote his startup. Eventually, he found himself engaging with other educators in a Twitter Chat called #EdChat.

#EdChat is a group of Twitter users who get together to discuss education, share ideas and learn from one another.

Zeb learned more in the three months he spent in #EdChat about education than he did in his four years of college, his year in the teaching credential program and his four years as a high school history teacher.

The #EdChat group is responsible for multiple Ted Talks, multiple books on education, and have changed the way children are educated in the United States.

This niche -- educators passionate about education and technology -- changed Zeb. By connecting with individuals who were just as passionate about a topic as he was, he became envigorated and worked harder to achieve more.

The golf niche can be just as powerful.

The Golf Niche

"Social media has been our forum for success."
— Ken Lee, Editor-in-Chief at Bunker's Paradise [20]

People who love and follow golf are a niche.

In 1996, Tiger Woods became a professional golfer. The buzz was incredible. When Zeb heard of his signing with Nike, he used his allowance to buy his first golf hat -- a black cap with a white Nike swoosh on the front -- his first golfing purchase.

---

20 "Defining Success Podcast." Defining Success Podcast. N.p., n.d. Web. 15 Feb. 2014.

Almost everyone was talking about Tiger Woods.

As Tiger Woods began winning, so did golf courses all over the country. People who never played golf before were taking up the game.

In 1995, before Tiger Woods turned pro, there were 16.4 million core golfers. In 2000, there were 19.7 million.

Why was there such a dramatic increase?

For a brief moment in history, golf was cool.

Tiger was winning and every major sports news outlet was covering his success. It was almost impossible to go a day without hearing Tiger Woods' name.

Golf grew. The public became fascinated with Tiger through word of mouth and everyone was talking about golf.

Word of Mouth on Steroids

In 2005, the number of core golfers dropped to 18.0 million, in 2010 it dropped to 14.8 million and again in 2011... to 14.4 million.

That's a 25% decrease since the peak of the Tiger phenomenon. Couple that with the fact they reconfigured what a core golfer is. A core golfer in 2000 was someone who played 24 rounds per year. Today, a core golfer is defined as playing eight rounds a year. [21]

Facebook launched in 2004, changing the way people consume information. Tiger's emergence on the golf scene came on the last wave of mass media, the last

---

21 "Session 101: Opening Keynote - State of the Golf Industry." Proc. of Crittenden Golf Conference, Phoenix.

time where public perception was controlled exclusively by newspapers, television, and radio. [22]

Now, most people are getting their information from social media.

Social media is word of mouth marketing on steroids.

For example, the average Facebook user is connected to 130 "friends." [23]

Golfers are more social. The average Facebook user connected to Los Serranos Country Club at the end of 2012 had 597 "friends."

If a user interacts with the Los Serranos Facebook page, that message has the potential to be sent out to all 597 "friends."

Another example: The Arroyo Trabuco Facebook page, which we've been managing for less than a year has 2,316 Facebook "Likes."

If a golfer connects with the Arroyo Trabuco Facebook page and says something nice about the course, that endorsement will reach -- on average -- their 597 Facebook friends.

Since Arroyo Trabuco is a social media savvy golf course, it multiplies that number by sharing golfer feedback with their 2,316 followers.

Golf courses with a strong social media presence have golfers saying great things about their courses daily and they have the opportunity to use those authentic messages to endorse their golf course.

The conventional wisdom that a happy customer tells a handful of people and an unhappy customer tells hundreds no longer applies. In today's social media world, a happy customer tells hundreds, an unhappy

---

22 "Facebook." Wikipedia. Wikimedia Foundation, 16 Jan. 2014. Web. 16 Jan 2014.

23 "Facebook Statistics." Statistic Brain RSS. N.p., n.d. Web. 15 Dec. 2013.

customer tells hundreds and a smart business shares happy customer experiences with thousands.

Our chapter on Reputation Management explains how to get those happy customers to talk more about your golf course and leverage those comments to build a strong reputation for your golf course.

Identify Your Ambassadors

Imagine your ideal customers.

- What traits do they possess?
- How do they talk about your golf course with others?
- How often do they play at your course?

When speaking with golf course owners and operators, they give us roughly the same answer: their ideal customers pay the rack rate, play multiple times a week, and play exclusively at their course.

Those customers are great.

However, our ideal customer is someone who does all those things -- and -- tells every single person they know how amazing our golf course is.

These "social golfers" are your biggest advocates.

Every golf course has dozens, if not hundreds of ambassadors willing to tell others about your golf course -- through social media -- if you create opportunities for them to do so.

What Golf Courses Need to Do to Stay Competitive

To thrive in the new economy, golf needs to entice golfers with pull marketing tactics, like social media, to grow as fast as other sports and recreational activities.

According to the 2013 Outdoor Research Participation Report by the Outdoor Foundation, golf dropped from 29,816,000 golfers (10.9% of the population) in 2006 to 22,442,000 golfers (7.8% of the population) in 2012.

To put that in perspective, yoga, an activity not even recognized by the 2006 report has gone from 17,758,000 (6.4% of the population in 2008) to 24,180,000 (8.4% of the population in 2012.[24]

As stewards of the game, it is our duty to get more people talking about the game -- through social media -- to share the joy, fulfillment and value golf creates.

Enable your "social golfers" to be ambassadors of the game. Motivate them to talk, discuss and interact with anything and everything golf. The responsibility of growing golf is now in the hands of local golf courses.

Discuss at SocialGolfCourse.com

Who is your ideal customer? How can you get them?

---

24 Outdoor Participation Report 2013. Rep. Outdoor Foundation, n.d. Web. 15 Feb. 2014.

CHAPTER 8

How Being Social Can Increase Profits at Your Course

*"How in the evening each dilates on his own
wonderful strokes, and the singular chances that
befell him -- all under the pleasurable delusion
that every listener is as interested in his game as
he himself is."* — St. Andrews Writer [25]

Golfers Are Using Social Media

Want to find out if golfers are using social media?
Just do a Facebook search for your golf course. It will tell you how many golfers have "Checked-In" to your golf course while using Facebook from their mobile phones.

According to MarketLand.com, on average, 10% of adults will "Check-In" to a location. Multiply the

---

25 Canfield, Jack. Chicken Soup for the Golfer's Soul: The 2nd Round: More Stories of Insight, Inspiration and Laughter on the Links. Deerfield Beach, FL: Health Communications, 2002. Print.

"Check-Ins" on your Facebook page by 10 to get an estimate of how many Facebook users are playing golf at your course. [26]

Arroyo Trabuco's Facebook page is three years old and has close to 10,000 "Check-Ins," while San Dimas Canyon Golf Course's Facebook is two years old and has about 7,000 "Check-Ins."

Both golf courses, then, had around 35,000 visitors per year who used Facebook.

These numbers do not include other social media platforms like Twitter, YouTube, LinkedIn, Pinterest, Instagram, Greenskeeper.org and others.

The actual number of golfers using social media (Facebook, Twitter and LinkedIn) was more than 71% in 2012, according to the National Golf Foundation . . . and that number is growing.[27]

Are golfers using social media?

You betcha.

Gaining Exposure: Is Social Media Marketing Better than Print, Radio and Television?

If you're spending money on print, radio, television or any other form of marketing -- before spending on social media -- you're not being effective. Just in terms of exposure, the benefits of social media marketing when comparing cost are better than print, radio and television.

Social media marketing is targeted, can reach more people, can reach them more often, and is less intrusive.

---

26 "Check-In Service Usage Has More Than Doubled In Past 9 Months, Study Says." Marketing Land. N.p., n.d. Web. 15 Feb. 2014.

27 "Golf Entrepreneur." : Core Golfers & Technology. N.p., n.d. Web. 15 Feb. 2014.

Below is an example from our client in 2012, Los Serranos Country Club, the California Golf Course of the Year, which we compared with advertising in the local newspaper and a Southern California golf magazine. Here were our findings:

Local Newspaper

Advantages - The newspaper circulation is large and geographically specific.

Disadvantages - The newspaper does not target golfers. The newspaper ad does not provide an opportunity for follow up. Newspaper circulations are declining.

- Circulation - 119,000
- Cost Per Ad (3 x 5) - $340
- Cost Per Thousand potential Impressions - $2.86

A Southern California golf magazine

Advantages: The golf magazine targets golfers.

Disadvantages: The golf magazine is not geographically specific as they marketed to golfers in a 200-plus mile area. The golf magazine ads did not provide an opportunity for follow up. Magazine circulations are declining.

- Circulation – 50,000
- Frequency – 2.5
- Impressions – 125,000
- Cost per Ad - $1,700
- Cost Per Thousand Impressions - $13.60

19th Hole Media (after 18 months of operation)

Advantages: Our social media campaign targets golfers. The golfers we target lived within a 50-mile radius making our ads geographically specific. Once a customer connected with our ad, they were typically exposed to our message more than 20 times per month.

Disadvantages: Social media exposure takes time to develop a loyal following, a consistent strategy and expertise.

*Our impact increased at a constant rate, if we were to work for another 18 months, our reach and impressions would double, but our cost per month would stay the same.

- Reach per Week- more than 77,136 people
- Frequency per Ad (once a day) – 2.9
- Impressions per Week - more than 282,270
- Cost Per Week - less than $250
- Cost Per Thousand Impressions - $0.88

Social media can reach a lot more people at a fraction of the cost of traditional marketing methods.

But, the advantages of social media don't stop there.

On Greenskeeper.org, more than 75% of the 100,000-plus monthly visitors do not go more than a day without visiting the site. As of October 30, 2013, Facebook had 1.19 billion monthly active users with 874 million mobile users and 728 million daily users.[28]

Not only are we reaching more customers, but we are reaching them more often. In some cases, golfers were seeing our posts more than 20 times per month. Com-

---

28   "Facebook Passes 1.19 Billion Monthly Active Users, 874 Million Mobile Users, and 728 Million Daily Users." TNW Network All Stories RSS. N.p., n.d. Web. 13 Jan. 2014.

pare that with a monthly magazine who reaches your customers once a month or a daily newspaper where readers, may or may not see and notice your advertisement.

Encourage Golfers to Play More Often:

When Zeb first began working for Los Serranos Country Club in 2011. One of the first persons to comment on our Facebook posts, was Tammera Roy, mother of Amanda Roy an 11-year old-golfer who recently took up the game by entering a junior tournament at the course. The mother, excited that her daughter enjoyed the game, liked us on Facebook and began commenting regularly.

In one post, I asked the question, "What would you like to see from our Facebook page?"

Tammera responded with "Photos and posts about your junior tournaments." The next day we gathered some photos and the first picture we posted was of Amanda Roy with a 2nd place trophy she had received in the tournament.

Amanda and Tammera were thrilled and even signed up for golf lessons from one of the professionals at the golf course. Amanda and her mom visited the golf course over a hundred times from 2011 to 2013.

Tammera regularly commented on our Facebook posts after our initial encounter and has been a huge advocate for the course. The recognition Amanda and Tammera received on the Facebook page was a determining factor in them choosing to stay and play at Los Serranos Country Club. More than a hundred rounds and thousands of dollars. And the best part is . . . her story is not unique. This is happening at golf courses all over the country, for those golf courses who are using social media to connect with golfers like Amanda.

Target Golfers in Your Geographical Region

Another advantage to social media marketing over print marketing is the highly-targeted nature of the promotion itself. Messages go out directly to golfers who: play your golf course; are friends of the people who do; or to specific parameters you set such as "golfers" who live within 50 miles of your golf course.

With print media, there are no opportunities for follow up. If a person does see and connect with your ad, they must be ready to make a purchase and/or take action right away. If not, you lose the value of the ad and may never acquire that customer.

With social media, when golfers connect with you, you have the ability to reach them with your marketing campaigns continually for as long as they are connected with your golf course.

The most overlooked and most valuable argument for the importance of social media over print media is the ability for immediate feedback.

How Social Media Can Help You Build a Better Business

"Social media is where this world is going and it's going to continue to grow." - Kate Hughes[29]

Social media offers direct access to the wants and needs of your customers.

---

29 Welborn, Zeb. "Defining Success Podcast." Defining Success Podcast. N.p., n.d. Web. 15 Feb. 2014.

Not sure when the best day to hold an event is? Ask for input from your golfers.

Thinking of changing your snack shop menu? Ask your customers.

Want to know how you can improve your course? Ask your customers.

Social media offers real time feedback to golf courses, who can then improve their courses to make it a better place to play for everyone.

Remember, customers have options. And they have the ability to see and understand what kind of golf course you are and how you treat your customers. Your customers are smart. They no longer just consider an ad in a magazine to determine if your golf course is a great place to play. They look to find out what people are saying in real-time conversations online to determine if your golf course is the right place for them.

Recently, I was discussing an advertisement Los Serranos Country Club had invested in with a local golf magazine with a major misspelling on the front of their ad. It had been running for a week. No ad viewer had contacted the golf course to make them aware of this major flaw. Nobody.

With social media, problems are identified immediately, in real-time. If a typo were to exist on our page, we could fix it immediately. If there was slow play out on the course, we could address those concerns. If our customer service was not up to par, we can be made aware of the problem and we fix it.

Social media can help us build a better business by listening to the needs of our customer and accommodating them.

How Can Social Media Increase Sales?

Evaluating the effectiveness of social media is tricky for marketers, just like tv, radio and newspaper ads. It's difficult to determine how much money is coming in as a result of your marketing efforts.

Social media has an edge over traditional ads on tv, radio and newspaper because it offers more in-depth analytical tools which can help give better insights into its effectiveness. However, those tools can not pinpoint every transaction influenced by social media.

Some golf course operators fell in love with the tee time wholesaler model because they could track how many rounds they were bringing to the golf course. In their desire for pinpointing every transaction, golf courses lost brand loyalty and gave up a portion of their business to tee time wholesalers.

Social media is common sense.

It helps your golf course stay in the "top of mind" of your customers, because you are sharing, talking and communicating about anything and everything golf.

Conversation between two golfers:
Golfer #1: What are you up to on Friday? Want to play some golf?
Golfer #2: I'm in. Where do you want to play?
Golfer #1: Let's play _____ ("top of mind" golf course)
Golfer #2: I'm in!

With social media you can make that "top of mind" golf course your golf course. In addition, you can encourage golfer #1 to ask that question more often by giving him information about your golf course every day through social media.

In preparation for this book, we asked several golfers the following question:

Does social media encourage you to play more golf?

And here is what two of them had to say (you can see more by visiting www.SocialGolfCourse.com):

> *"Ever since I joined Los Serranos's Facebook page I felt I had the inside scoop. Its been roughly a year since adding Los Serranos to my "likes" list and in that time I've played 5 rounds (never as a single) at the Country Club. Traditionally I will play maybe 2 total rounds per year at the course because of where I live. Their Facebook page does a great job keeping it's fans updated with course conditions, deals, and updates on current events evolving around the world golf and Los Serranos. Furthermore, Zeb has connected with the Los Serranos family of players by asking us to share our experiences as it pertains to LSCC. (i.e. What's your favorite hole? Scores over the weekend? etc.) It not only gives the players the opportunity to interact with management, it allows for players to interact with one another."*

— Los Serranos Golfer, Tom Robinson

At Los Serranos, Tom Robinson did not comment every day. He was not particularly active like many other Facebook followers. Yet, Tom sent us this email to let us know the type of increase in rounds he experienced being exposed to the Los Serranos Country Club Facebook page.

In his estimation, he played three more rounds in 2012 than any year previously. He played 2.5 times more. And he never played alone, bringing guests each time he played. Assuming Tom had a full foursome each time he played, social media contributed to an increase of 12 rounds of golf in 2012.

In one week, from January 8 - January 14, 2014 Arroyo Trabuco had 1,020 people talking about Arroyo Trabuco Golf Club on Facebook, just like Tom Robinson did at Los Serranos Country Club back in 2012. If every one of those golfers contributed toward an increase in 12 rounds . . . an increase in 12,000 rounds per year for Arroyo Trabuco Golf Club.

Of course not every golfer will produce that kind of increase in rounds, but some will. And others will produce more.

Another endorsement:

> *"Social media is directly responsible for my increasing knowledge about golf. I was a rank beginner when I first found GK. Finding GK ... motivated me to look for a few more sites specifically targeting women golfers so I wouldn't feel so all alone. ... Learning about golf in a friendly, non-critical environment was super important to how much golf I played and play! ... Finding friends to golf with through social media was even MORE important. Many women, myself included, are very hesitant to go to courses when starting out. Making friends online gave me just that extra boost of courage to get myself going ...*

Second, knowing what to expect both from other golfers and from the courses I wanted to play alleviated a lot of stress which, especially in the beginning, allowed me to feel more excited and less nervous about playing. THAT translated into many more happy rounds!

AND then... just the conversation about golf that happens on social media sites keeps my mind on golf even when I'm not on the course. The few sites that were targeted mostly at women were very very busy. There was always something happening. New threads and new comments everyday. Lots of ways to get involved with a golf community ...

The community that has grown up around GK makes golf so much more fun and interesting- and yeah, I sure do play more because of it!!"

— GK'er Chris Pennington

These examples illustrate the potential of social media. These golfers played more golf and encouraged others to play more golf. Without engaging on social media, these golfers might have tried another recreational activity. They chose golf because local golf courses and Greenskeeper.org made a connection with them.

A connection on social media that makes sense.

Pico Rivera Golf Course: A Social Golf Experiment

While writing this book, Zeb's father, Larry came across an article written in the January, 2014 issue of Southland Golf Magazine titled, Pico Rivera Getting Back on Track by Michael Lednovich. The article spoke of Pico Rivera Golf Course which, two years ago was costing the city $300,000 per year to maintain.[30]

Pico Rivera Golf Club is a prime example of what can happen when a golf course becomes a social golf course. In two years, they went from averaging 119 to 190 daily rounds, a 159.7% increase.

Zeb spoke with Scott Williams, Golf Course Superintendent, Larry Taylor, from GolfLinks Management LLC and James Ochs, Director of Golf about the turnaround at Pico Rivera Golf Course.

"Golf is definitely a social game," Williams said.

The turnaround focused on customer service and golf course conditions. The team worked to make sure they got to know their customers and greeted them professionally. They cultivated a professional teaching staff, and hosted more banquets and golf tournaments.

They collaborated with the city to make sure Pico Rivera Golf Course was something the city could be proud of.

They sent out personalized email blasts, developed a Facebook presence and communicated specials and upcoming events to their patrons and community members.

"Social media is a key component in the golf industry and word of mouth helps you or hurts you," Williams said.

---

30 Lednovich, Michael. "COURSES." COURSES. Southland Golf, n.d. Web. 15 Feb. 2014.

And they worked to build positive word of mouth.

Pico Rivera Golf Course represents the potential value of turning your golf course into a social golf course.

"We don't see this as a golf course, we view it as a community asset ... It's not one thing we did to turn this golf course around. It was all the little things," Taylor said.

What is the Return on Investment (ROI) of Social Media?

One common question I get regarding social media is what is the return on investment?

Gary Vaynerchuk, a social media guru and author of Crush It, frequently gets asked this question.

His response is almost always, "What is the ROI of your mom?"

When Zeb was in the first grade, his mother would leave little presents in the lunch she made for him before he went to school. One day, he opened his lunch to find a tiny bear with a heart on its chest, emblazoned across the heart were the words, "You're Special!" As a child growing up, his mom continued to reinforce the concept and he believes he's special.

Can Zeb track the value or the ROI of his mother? He can try. He can look back at all the things he has done that have come from believing he's special, but it is not the complete picture.

When Gary responds to people who ask him what the ROI of his mother is, he responds, "It's ****** everything!"

Social media is the same way.

You can work in systems to analyze and track your ROI and you can do a good job on determining some ways business has come to you from having a strong social media presence, but it will never tell the complete picture.

For those golf courses that become social golf courses, they will understand they can't evaluate their social media presence on ROI alone because to a golf course, social media is "******* everything!"

As the host of the Defining Success Podcast Zeb has interviewed more than 50 successful people, including several best-selling authors, a Pulitzer prize-winning photographer, several multi-millionaire entrepreneurs, a world-famous tennis coach, two golf course general managers and recipients of the California Golf Course of the Year, nationally recognized educators and others.

Throughout his interviews with successful people common themes have emerged. One of the most prominent themes is almost every successful person has identified a goal not connected to money. Successful people learn how to be of service to others and financial benefits come to them as a result.

If you're evaluating your business decisions strictly on the ROI, you may miss out on opportunities to benefit and grow your business.

In Zeb's interview with Chris Brogan, the CEO and President of Human Business Works, an education publishing and media company, he said, "When I think of ways to make money, I fail. When I think of ways to serve people, I make money."

The motto for my internet marketing business, Welborn Media, is "Share Your Passion. Grow Your Business."

We don't want to work with businesses who are looking to get a "return on investment." Because to evaluate ROI is to focus solely on numbers. Business is done between people. A balance sheet, while helpful, can never replace human interaction. We choose to work with businesses who are working to serve their community because those businesses will be the ones who succeed in our social economy.

Another reason we work with passionate business owners is because those business owners are our biggest advocates. They are more connected. They have more friends, family and influence. We know that by being of service to them . . . they are going to sell our services to their family, friends, colleagues, neighbors, acquaintances and anybody else who is willing to listen.

And golf course operators should desire the same of their golfers.

They should want to attract golfers who are so passionate about the game they are willing to promote your golf course to their family, friends, colleagues, neighbors, acquaintances and anybody else who is willing to listen.

Golfers all over the internet are waiting to act as your word-of-mouth marketing team. Give them the opportunity.

Discuss at SocialGolfCourse.com

How has social media impacted your relationship with your customers? Share your stories with us!

CHAPTER 9

How to Become a Social Golf Course

*"If you don't have four hours three to four times
a month to enjoy a game of golf with your friends
than your life is not balanced."* — Jay Miller[31]

The National Golf Foundation estimated there are
25.7 million golfers in the U.S. in 2011 and only 1.7
million have a USGA handicap. That is 24 million golfers -- over 90% -- enjoying the game casually instead of
competitively.[32]

Do you think the more social your golf course is, the
more it's going to appeal to the majority of golfers? The
answer is yes.

The first step to becoming a social golf course is to
establish a social culture at your golf course that can
be reflected online. This means customer service that
brings value through directly engaging golfers in a
cheerful, professional way.

31 Welborn, Zeb. "Defining Success Podcast." Defining Success Podcast. N.p.,
n.d. Web. 15 Feb. 2014.

32 "Session 101: Opening Keynote - State of the Golf Industry." Proc. of Crittenden Golf Conference, Phoenix.

When you think of your online presence, think of it as an extension of your business. Being social online but not providing a social golf experience at your course is counter productive.

How can golf courses create a social culture and match it with their online presence to retain more customers and bring in more business?

The Website

Your website is your online marketing home. Everything you do online should direct everyone back to your website where you can include actions items like signing up for an e-mail list, booking tee times, signing up for programs, booking tournaments and contacting your staff.

It should be your main information hub allowing visitors to get to know you.

Golfers visit a website because it is the most trusted place to get information from the golf course itself.

So, maintaining a visually appealing, easy to navigate and interactive website is critical.

Email List/Newsletter

Golf courses should have an email marketing campaign in place.

We'd recommend offering incentives to customers in order to build your branded, self-developed, home-course email lists. We don't think it's a good idea to trade or pay for emails: it is often considered spam and could damage your reputation

One way to build your branded email database is to offer discounted rounds on customers birthdays, contests, special offers and informational newsletters.

All e-mails you send to your subscribers should be relevant. When cultivating an e-mail list, do your best to gather information about each customer and target your group emails appropriately.

Send your e-mail newsletters regularly, updating your golfers on course conditions, providing golf tips and sharing events or tournaments. Golf courses that use their email newsletters strictly as a sales tool with push messaging are being ignored by the majority of your golfers. A clever headline and meaningful content will help increase the open rates of your emails and get more of your golfers to take action on your requests.

It's important to convey the right message to your golfers. Here is how an example of how an email marketing campaign can enhance your reputation or tarnish it:

> *"I have to admit that the BEST emails really get me excited about playing the courses who send them. I LOVE the humor in the emails from Champions at the Retreats- and they have me jonesing to play the course even if it IS hard. :-) By the same token Tukwet Canyon's constant emails telling me what they are serving in their clubhouse, with hardly anything ever mentioned about GOLF, turn me off to the course every time. (and I LOVE Legends!) I have written them and asked them to only send golf related emails as I am not interested in special dinner offers.... but that has apparently fallen on deaf ears. A real faux pas as far as I'm concerned and one that does cost them my business.*

An update. Last night they sent me YET ANOTHER email about a Valentine's Day Dinner...with nothing in the entire email about golf. I unsubbed from their email list. This means I won't see any golf specials they MIGHT send so I won't take advantage of them which means I won't play there as often. I was also debating on joining their newly formed Women's Club but won't do that now either. They are losing revenue over this- which they know since I wrote them and told them why!"

— GK'er Chris Pennington

Mention specials and sales but don't do it exclusively through email.

Once you've created a social culture at your golf course, incorporate social into your newsletter.

- For example, you could:
- Summarize popular Facebook posts and link to them
- Give readers a schedule of upcoming blog posts
- Encourage participation on social platforms
- Notify readers of specials, contests and other social events

Lastly, find ways to feature your customers and their opinions in your newsletter, which can lead to open discussion and debate. It will convey appreciation towards your customers that will not go unnoticed.

Facebook

Facebook is the best resource for any business with a clearly identifiable target market. Through Facebook advertising, it's easy to reach out to people who identify themselves as golfers within a 50-mile radius of your course. It allows you to reach golfers more effectively than traditional marketing.

With Facebook, you have the opportunity to reach golfers every time they log-in. Unlike newspapers or magazine advertising, you'll be reaching your customers daily, making them a part of your golfing community.

Blog

Golf courses should see themselves as the central hub of their communities. Newspapers are suffering, while citizen blogs are becoming more influential. A blog, therefore, can be used as the "newspaper" of your golf course, highlighting events, updating members and sharing stories. If you are unsure of what to put on your blog, we'll have you covered in our chapter on content creation.

A blog can be a vital tool to encourage, promote and retain tournaments, banquets and events.

Twitter

Twitter is great as a listening tool.

Golfers frequently share their experiences on Twitter and golf courses have the ability to interact with them.

It's easy to identify golfers on Twitter because they mention they enjoy golf in their searchable Twitter profiles. Golf courses can reach out to these golfers, develop relationships and entice them to play at their course.

While working at San Dimas Canyon Golf Course, Zeb reached out to a group called Bunkers Paradise. Bunkers Paradise is an active, social, online golfing community here in Southern California. Bunkers Paradise was looking to hold a golf tournament. Because of our relationship on Twitter, they chose San Dimas Canyon Golf Course.

The Bunkers Paradise Charity golf tournament benefitting the Special Olympics was sponsored by Cleveland Golf, Nike Golf, La Quinta Resort, I Need the Ball, Routine Golf Gear, New York Life - Covina Valley, Jay Lim Golf Academy, Froh Chiropractic, Marc Pro, Dixon Golf, The Earl Family, Best Grips, HG Group, Greystar Products and Robert Brey. The tournament would not have happened at San Dimas without Twitter.

Golf courses can also search for people who use particular terms on Twitter, including golf courses by name. A quick Twitter search can identify Twitter users who recently visited your golf course.

If a Twitter user shares they had a great time at your course: say thank you.

If a Twitter user shares they played another local course: ask about their round.

If a Twitter user plays your golf course regularly: engage them.

YouTube

The possibilities of YouTube are endless.

Make a commercial for your course and share it with your golfers. Highlight achievements of golfers at your course. Read our chapter on content creation to get more ideas on ways you can use YouTube to encourage golfers to play more often.

Instagram

Recently, we've noticed increased involvement for golfers and golf courses on Instagram. In today's society, more people are accessing information on their mobile phones and Instagram is leading the way in visual content consumed through smart phones.

Not only is Instagram "the" social platform for the younger generation, it is becoming increasingly popular for golf.

Most golf courses are loaded with 1000's of beautiful picture taking opportunities. Smartphone cameras make it easier than ever to take photos worth sharing. For a golfer, every golf course photo is a point of discussion.

Instagram's hashtags (#s) make it easy for any golf course to find photos about its course and promote those photos. Currently, the hashtag, #golfcourse has more than 200,000 photos, #golf has 2.8 million and #golfing has 250,000.

If your goal is to target younger golfers, try Instagram.

Pinterest, Vine, Google+, etc.: Your Outreach/Listening Tools

Social media is constantly evolving and each platform will offer different ways to reach out and encourage your golfers to play at your golf course.

Visit SocialGolfCourse.com to stay up to date on different social media platforms and the best ways golf courses can use those platforms.

Discuss at SocialGolfCourse.com

Which platform is the most important for golf courses to utilize to reach more customers?

CHAPTER 10

Greenskeeper.org Golf's Social Network

"When a golf course is being authentic and thankful, golfers will see that as that's how they treat their customers." — John Hakim[33]

Greenskeeper.org was launched in 2002 and has built up a loyal user base of over 64,000 golfers. Golfers use Greenskeeper.org to help them decide where to play and engage each other socially.

Greenskeeper.org's mission statement is "To help golfers enjoy their golf experiences as much as possible." It has been steadfast with this mission statement for over 10 years as well as aligning itself with its registered trademark "Know Before You Go."

As of 2014 golfers have posted over 40,000 reviews, rated over 37,000 golf courses and posted close to 20,000 golf course photos on Greenskeeper.org. This informa-

---

33 Welborn, Zeb. "Defining Success Podcast." Defining Success Podcast. N.p., n.d. Web. 15 Feb. 2014.

tion is widely used by site users to make decisions about where to play golf.

Greenskeeper.org membership is still growing and its golf course coverage expanding. Currently, the website covers AZ, CA, CO, FL, HW, NM, OR, TX, UT and WA. If your golf course is listed on Greenskeeper.org, it will have a unique page where it can engage golfers, submit photos, post playing tips, read/write reviews and read/submit ratings.

The heart of Greenskeeper.org is its loyal community of avid golfers called GK'ers. GK'ers make up about 10% of the site's 60,000-plus membership and account for the majority of golf course reviews, golf course ratings, forum posts, social interaction, outing attendance and word of mouth marketing. The content produced from GK'ers is what attracts the 150,000-plus monthly visitors who account for the 1,000,000-plus monthly pageviews on Greenskeeper.org.

More than 75% of all visitors to Greenskeeper.org revisit the site within 24 hours.

With their postings, GK'ers have established themselves as authentic voices golfers have come to trust.

In the book, *The Tipping Point* by Malcolm Gladwell, GK'ers would be synonymous with Mavens. Mavens are "information specialists" or "people we rely on to connect us with new information." So a golf course's goal when building an active presence on Greenskeeper.org is not appealing to the masses, but appealing to GK'ers. Because GK'ers will connect the masses to the information.

Before going into how to best reach GK'ers and other beneficial techniques on Greenskeeper.org, John would like to share some data comparing two media buy campaigns on Greenskeeper.org to illustrate the power of engagement.

On Greenskeeper.org the primary media buy is called Golf Course Integration Packages. The goal of the Golf Course Integration Packages is to extend a golf course's online presence directly onto Greenskeeper.org by integrating it into Greenskeeper.org's core content. A few ways Greenskeeper.org measures the effectiveness of campaigns is by the amount of page views a client's golf course(s) pages receives, booking link clicks and reviews.

In this comparison Client A has an active presence on Greenskeeper.org. They maintain their profile page, thank members who leave reviews, engage in forums, donate prizes to Greenskeeper.org outings and respond quickly to all private messages.

Client A also has booking links, specials, beautiful photos, coupons, social media links and an active Facebook Like Box feed integrated into its course pages.

Client B has booking links, specials, and a Facebook Like Box integrated onto its course pages. Yet, most photos are old, the Facebook Like Box is not active, they do not have a profile page, they do not thank site members that post reviews and they do not engage site members.

Client B posts only hard sale offers instead of trying to engage users on the Greenskeeper.org platform. Although Client B still achieves adequate ROI through well performing booking links to justify its campaign, they missed out on the campaigns potential to create word of mouth marketing through reviews and page views.

Client A:
Page Views: 11,585
Booking Link Clicks: 352
Reviews: 28

Client B:
Page Views: 5,777
Booking Link Clicks: 368
Reviews: 14

Why did Client B stick with its approach?

Because Client B continued to treat a social marketing platform like a traditional print or e-mail marketing platform. Client B, like many advertisers, failed to recognize the value of the extra work it takes to engage on social platforms. To get the most out of any social media campaign, engagement is critical.

Greenskeeper.org has not launched its mobile application social network platform yet. The mobile application platform is estimated to be launched in June 2014 and will provide many additional ways to implement social media.

How can your golf course take advantage of Greenskeeper.org?

There are two ways a golf course can use Greenskeeper.org: the free version and an affordable Golf Course Integration media buy between $50 and $300 per month.

Using Greenskeeper.org for Free

Step #1:

Join Greenskeeper.org.

For a username, we recommend using your first name-course name. For example: Mark-LosAngelesGC.

When the golf course starts engaging Greenskeeper.org site users, site users immediately know they are communicating with a staff member from the golf course. The first name creates a human connection and it's recommended multiple golf course staff join Greenskeeper.org in the same manner.

Greenskeeper.org is a specific niche platform where advertisers can reach core golfers every day. When the Greenskeeper.org app is launched the Summer of 2014, users will be able to join and integrate with their Facebook accounts.

Step #2:

Create a profile page.

You will be able access your profile page from your MyGK page. Spend a little time filling out your profile. When you make contact with a user, the first thing they will likely do is check out your profile page. Make sure it represents your golf course the way you want it to.

Step #3:

Visit your golf course page on Greenskeeper.org and thank every person who posted a review within the last 12 months.

While logged into Greenskeeper.org an icon envelope appears next to the reviewing member's name. Clicking on the icon will take you to the message center. Send them a message thanking them for posting a positive or informative review. Be sure to introduce yourself and make a reference to something about the review.

If the review is negative, still reach out to the reviewer and ask them about the issues they had and how you can make their next experience more enjoyable. More on this topic will be covered in our chapter on Reputation Management.

Step #4:

Go to the Greenskeeper.org forums.

Search for your golf course to find discussions about it. Reply to any forum topics mentioning your golf course. This will immediately push that discussion to the top of the homepage and community page.

In addition to joining user discussions referencing your golf course, join in on other conversations of interest. This helps create a connection between you and other members of Greenskeeper.org so that when you engage with them, they will be more apt to pay attention.

Step #5:

Make sure the content on your golf course page is up-to-date and authentic.

Look through the photos posted of your course and update them if necessary. Add captions to the photos to make them easier to find in search engines and to enhance the user experience. Use authentic photos and not stock media photos.

Once your photos are uploaded they will be reviewed by Greenskeeper.org content management for quality control. If any photo is low quality, it will be rejected. Snap photos of your clubhouse, practice facilities, and anything you feel would be valuable to golfers.

Make sure your scorecard is up-to-date and e-mail golf@greenskeeper.org of any changes that need to be made. You can also post hole-by-hole playing tips for your course. We recommend having this done by someone who is very familiar with playing your course, typically the head pro.

Step #6:

Become a GK'er.

When you play a golf course, share your experience. Be a contributor. Become a leader. Greenskeeper.org has 60,000-plus members. The more active you are, the more likely site users will see you as a credible voice.

Step #7:

Organize an outing.

Perhaps the best way to connect with GK'ers is to arrange to spend time with them at your course -- or even tee it up. Having a few GK'ers as advocates will be worth it.

Greenskeeper.org is a Media Buy

Golf courses can consider boosting their presence on Greenskeeper.org by purchasing a Golf Course Integration package for as little as $50 per month.

Greenskeeper.org has over 30 golf course clients and has been producing effective measurable campaign results for golf courses for over eight years.

Greenskeeper.org works with golf courses by integrating booking links, special offers, coupons, photo links, Facebook feeds and other means to drive business.

To get more information on golf course client campaigns please contact Greenskeeper.org - advertising@ greenskeeper.org.

* Easter Egg - If you're a golf course owner or operator, contact Greenskeeper.org via e-mail to advertising@greenskeeper.org with the subject line GK Easter Egg to qualify to win a free 3-month level 2 Golf Course Integration media buy on Greenskeeper.org. Include your name, position and contact information. Greenskeeper, LLC will select one winner in September 2014 for a campaign to run October, November and December of 2014. *

Discuss at SocialGolfCourse.com

How do I get more GK'ers playing my golf course?

More ideas!

CHAPTER 11

Creating Content to Build a Golf Community

By now, we hope you understand that social media is important. You know you need to help build a social community at your course. But, how do you use it? How do you get people talking about your golf course using social media? What could you write, photograph or tweet to get golfers excited about your golf course?

Creating content for social media is not easy, but we've worked in the industry long enough to create content that will resonate with your golfers.

Micro content is smaller pieces of content used to post on social sites like Facebook, Twitter, Instagram and most other social media platforms. They are short questions, comments or quips designed to engage followers.

Macro content is larger pieces of content designed to educate, entertain, or help to tell the story of a golf course.

Macro Content

Macro content can be described as larger pieces that take more than a paragraph to articulate. Macro content is great for storytelling, to bolster a unique selling proposition and to offer value to your golfers. Macro content can also be broken into smaller pieces which golf courses can use to post as micro content on their other platforms.

Hole in One Stories

A hole in one is one of the greatest achievements a person can have in any sport, and it's also one of the rarest. Golf courses can capitalize on this opportunity by documenting the event.

In 1999, Zeb's brother Rocky (14 years old at the time), teed it up on a downhill 351-yard par 4 at Los Serranos Country Club. He reached back and walloped a screaming line drive shot down the center of the fairway. The ball rolled between two bunkers just in front of the green hit the pin and dropped in the hole for an ace!

When he came to the ProShop to announce his miraculous feat, the golf professional seemed unimpressed and handed him a standard form to fill out which he would then have to mail to receive a plaque he'd have to pay for. No announcement was made and the excitement of the hole in one at this golf course died.

Opportunity missed.

One of the best things to encourage word of mouth and build excitement at your golf course is to share in the success of the golfers who play your course.

A hole in one should be celebrated. Imagine the next time a golfer gets a hole in one at your course, you announce his name over the loudspeakers to let everyone at the course know about his feat. You take down the golfers phone number and email address so you can have your social media manager interview him for a story about his/her hole in one. You take a picture with the golfer at the hole where he recorded his ace. You then share his/her story with all visitors who come to your website, in your email newsletter, on a bulletin board at your golf course, with the golfer himself and maybe even the local newspaper.

A social golf course would never miss out on that opportunity to promote golf. People love sharing and talking about a hole in one and the more you introduce these stories of success to your golfers, the more likely they are to share, discuss and talk about your golf course.

Not only that, but the golfer will feel special. The more people we can recognize, the more likely they are to continue to play and promote golf.

19th Hole Stories

One of Zeb's favorite things to do is listen to golf stories or, as he prefers to call them, 19th hole stories. 19th hole stories are the stories your golfers share while they are in the clubhouse before and after their round.

Golfers tell 19th hole stories because they have an emotional attachment to them. Many golfers keep coming back to your course, knowing the next 19th hole story is just a round of golf away. Sharing 19th hole stories via your website, newsletter, blog or on social media will develop a much stronger appreciation and attachment to your golf course.

As with hole in one stories, 19th hole stories are shareable, which are great for social media. If you've ever played golf at a course regularly, you know certain holes bring up memories and shareable experiences which enhance the golf round.

Every time I reach the tee box where my brother got his hole in one, I tell my playing partners about it. Sharing 19th hole stories will substantially increase the word of mouth experience at your golf course, online and away from your course.

To get content for your 19th hole stories, just ask your golfers.

While working at Los Serranos Country Club, Zeb reached out to golfers via Facebook to ask if anyone was willing to share their 19th hole stories and a local golfer named Bob Pouliot replied. Over the next year, Bob wrote story after story about his greatest experiences at Los Serranos Country Club. He shared these stories with his family and friends and they began to organize weekly outings to the local course consisting of between four and six groups.

The value of 19th hole stories didn't stop there. The golfers who read these 19th hole stories are reminded of the experiences they've had at your golf course and for those who maybe have not frequented your course, they develop a sense of what it is like to be a golfer there.

For example, here's a story my Dad tells about playing golf with his Uncle Earl, and everytime he tells it, he talks about the golf course where it all happened.

> *"Uncle Earl was playing a round at Whittier Narrows when he and his foursome came up to a par 3 tee box. The tee shot required a 5-iron over a wide, concrete-lined culvert. The group in front waved us up and Uncle Earl was first to tee it up. He swung hard, kinda topped it into the culvert.*

As amazing as it may be, his Top Flight bounced off the bottom of the culvert, into the side and then straight back at him. He caught it in mid-air, calmly leaned over and placed it back on the tee.

Well, we were busting a gut laughing, but the group on the green didn't know what happened until we finally joined them on the green. They thought Uncle Earl performed some kind of trick shot.

I'll always think about Earl's amazing shot every time I think about Whittier Narrows."

To encourage golfers to play more often at your golf course, get them emotionally invested. Share the great experiences golfers have at your golf course with others. The 19th hole isn't just a great way to relax after a round . . . it's a great way to increase word of mouth at your golf course.

Golf Tips and Lessons

Golf professionals are always looking for new golfers for lessons. Social media provides an opportunity for them ... to build credibility and connect with customers.

Beginning golfers can be introduced to the game, golf professionals can make money and you can make your golf course friendly and approachable.

The best way to improve is to get lessons from a professional, but often times, golfers fail to take lessons because they don't know how to go about it.

By sharing tips and ideas on ways to improve their golf game online, golfers will be able to get a feel for the expertise of a golf professional and choose a pro they can connect with. Ultimately, it makes golfers interested in signing up for lessons at your course.

Blog articles, newsletters and instructional videos are a great way to build the reputation of your golf professionals, your golf staff and your entire golf course.

Course Conditions

Many golfers obsess about the conditions of golf courses. Greenskeeper.org receives thousands of ratings and reviews on golf courses across the country.

By informing customers about the condition of your course, you are being upfront and honest. If course conditions are not up to par, you have the opportunity -- with social media -- to let customers know ahead of time.

Failing to inform a customer about the aeration schedule at your golf course could turn a customer away and could damage your relationship with your golfers.

It's not just the negatives you can deal with through social media, you can also talk about the positives -- like course improvement projects.

Giving golfers information about conditions is a great insiders access tool. The work superintendents do at golf courses is amazing and sharing what is done with your golfers will give them an opportunity to see, understand and appreciate their efforts.

In return, golfers can and will tell other golfers why there may be a trouble area on your course and, what's being done about it, and any improvements underway. It's a great word of mouth tool while your golfers are playing the golf course.

An example:

Buenaventura Golf Course Leverages GK

In early 2012 Buenaventura Golf Course had problems with the turf condition on eight of its fairways.

Greenskeeper.org Reviews:

> *"Sadly, this is probably the worst condition I have ever seen Buena in.... Numerous fairway sections need attention. For a flat course, there were several sections that were soggy/waterlogged, yet many sections were downright hard pan. Tough to chip around many holes with nothing but hard pan lies short of most greens."*

> *"Course conditions were not very good. Dry fairways and brown, some wet spots with mud. Chipping areas soggy and muddy."*

> *"The fairways were at times lush and in some areas had lots of bare spots, mud and major divots. Hole number 10 had the worst fairway conditions. Fairway on this hole was very bumpy, had so many bare spots, and lots of mud in other areas. The other fairways were not as bad as hole #10."*

Buenaventura Golf Course was well aware of the struggles it was having at the time and already made plans to do a major fairways re-sodding project in the Spring of 2012. The golf course also knew its reputation had been tarnished. But they were confident the re-sodded fairways would make a huge immediate improvement.

What the golf course did next was genius.

Buenaventura Golf Course, familiar with Greenskeeper.org, knew the best approach to getting the message out about the improved fairways.

The golf course contacted Greenskeeper.org in the spring to organize a small outing to take place soon after the re-sodding. Buenaventura could have waited for positive reviews about its fairways to be posted, but instead it was proactive. Results were fantastic.

The reviews came in:

> *"I was very impressed with the new Paspalum fairways on holes 1, 2, 8, 10, 12 and 15. Huge improvement to those previously troubled fairways. Massive improvement to hole 10."*

> *"Conditions for Buena were very good. They have resurfaced 8 fairways here and you can tell. Fairways were thick, lush and green with very little roll."*

> *"Conditions were nice overall and from what I hear, a vast improvement compared to what it used to be like out there before they redid many of the fairways recently."*

Before inviting a foursome out and having a small Greenskeeper.org outing Buenaventura Golf Course had only three reviews (all negative) for 2012. Soon after the course had 15 positive reviews.

The word was out and play was increasing.

Becoming a Golf Professional

Many golfers with skills dream about playing professionally, but the path is not easy. Most need help and information to help them go down that path. A how-to guide about how to become a golf professional could encourage golfers to play more often and contribute socially to your golf course.

The more golfers you bring into your sphere of influence, the more your network will expand. As your network expands, more and more golfers will be exposed to your course.

One of the most important things the golf industry can do is help young golfers succeed. Our greatest opportunity lies with juniors and their willingness to play and promote the game. Young golf professionals can be seen by their peers as role models. We need to give them exposure, build their self-esteem and give opportunities to share their experience with peers.

By documenting the journey of becoming a golf professional, we are validating their path and creating golfers a younger generation can look up to. The more young people who think golf is cool the more buzz we can generate about golf.

Pro Shop Merchandise

It's not just about greens fees. Social media can also illustrate discounts, bargains, new equipment, the hot driver, the cool putter. Make this content shareable and give your golfers a reason to come to your course.

Complete Your Foursome

What's one of the best way to build rapport with your golfers?

Play golf with them.

A member of your staff can play in a group with three other golfers, interview them throughout the round, share and listen to stories, take pictures and shoot video, all of which will be posted.

Then, at the end of the round, you can encourage the golfers to leave a review on Greenskeeper.org. You can then roll over those stories in your newsletter, blog, or other social media platforms.

Then, share these publicly. Those golfers have the opportunity to share the article with their friends and family through their own social media network. Social media networking leads to more networking. Word of mouth spreads.

At Arroyo Trabuco Golf Club, we posted a contest where the first golfer to respond to our Facebook post won a free round of golf for him and a friend at the golf course.

The winner was James Tony Juarez, who invited professional wrestler, Chavo Guerrero.

During the round of golf we took pictures and video.

Chavo then shared the experience with his 353,700-plus Twitter followers. Arroyo Trabuco received significant exposure that day. Chavo continues to play Arroyo Trabuco Golf Club, tweets about Arroyo Trabuco and engages on the Arroyo Trabuco Facebook page.

Social media networking leads to more networking. Word of mouth spreads.

At San Dimas Canyon Golf Course, we ran the same contest and Ron Bayless, a real estate agent for RE/

MAX responded to the post. We included the pictures and video of Ron on our social media platforms.

A short time later, San Dimas sought someone to invest in an advertisement to appear on scorecards for the golf course.

Guess who paid for the ad space on the score-cards? That's right -- RE/MAX agent, Ron Bayless.

When you share events, you are also sharing the stories with other potential golfers. These golfers can appreciate the unique culture at your golf course: a culture they might want to join.

Golfer Spotlight

Another good way to promote community at your course is to highlight the best golfers who play there.

One example:

In January 2014, Michael Block, the head professional at Arroyo Trabuco Golf Club, qualified for the Farmer's Insurance Open at Torrey Pines. We kept the Arroyo Trabuco faithful up-to-date on Michael's status in the tournament. Arroyo Trabuco Facebook followers supported him heavily on our Facebook page, some even making the trip to San Diego to watch the event.

During the tournament, where Block competed against guys like Phil Mickelson and Tiger Woods, we had some of the highest engagement we've had on the Arroyo Trabuco Facebook page. Arroyo Trabuco golfers knew Michael and were eager to support him and his efforts at the event.

Another example:

Up-and-coming pro Justin Itzen honed his game on the driving range at Los Serranos Country Club. The Los Serranos faithful continue to follow his exploits. They watched him make a run at qualifying for the

PGA in December 2013, and his progress on the Web. com tour.

Support your great golfers and let your customers know you give recognition to golfers who play your course.

Interviews

Conducting an interview is an easy way to create content for your golf course. Find someone with a compelling story and share their successes.

Zeb's Defining Success Podcast, launched in March, 2013 has introduced him to more than 50 successful people. Every one of those interviewees now knows him personally and his name recognition has become much higher as a result. Many of his interview subjects hired him, worked with him, or referred business to him.

In fact, the book you are reading came about because of an interview Zeb did with the owner of Greenskeeper. org, John Hakim.

Conducting interviews and featuring those dialogues on your blog, newsletter and social media outlets can provide a personal connection to the golf course.

Guest Posts

Another way to generate buzz and make people feel they are a part of your golf course is to give them an opportunity to write guest posts. A lot of people fancy themselves as writers and often get a kick out of seeing their names published.

Your audience is very specific and targeted. By creating an audience that can present their opinions and stories, you can get the attention of others with similar interest. A lot of people want to get in front of the golf course audience.

Local businesses can promote their products and services to your email list, your Facebook page, or your blog. Build up a large enough following and you can use your social reach as an added benefit to businesses looking to use your facilities for a banquet or a tournament. Or you could sell advertising space to businesses trying to reach people connected to you.

Membership Promotion

Earlier, we discussed the importance of creating a community where people feel appreciated, informed and involved. Giving people in your membership programs the opportunity to utilize your Facebook, email or online audience is a great way to build a community. And establishing a strong social community would encourage more people to sign up for those membership programs.

Tournament Promotion

Promoting tournaments through your blog and emails has many benefits. Often, golfers introduced to your course through a tournament will revisit.

By sharing golf tournaments on your blog you give people the opportunity to learn more about your golf course.

For example:

In August, 2011 Los Serranos Country Club promoted Phil Roche's Inland Valley Amateur Golf Tournament at their course. Visitors to the Los Serranos website increased by 600% during the tournament.

When the golf course promotes an outside golf tournament, it looks fantastic to tournament organizers, who are often the decision-makers in any organization.

Looking for a way to promote your golf course with tournament organizers?

Tell them you'll be sending out their tournament sign up forms and information through your email list.

If your list gets big enough you can consider having tournaments pay an extra fee to advertise their golf tournament to your email list, Facebook page and social media platforms. As a result, tournaments could even offset the cost for your content creation activities.

To promote a tournament, have your content creator interview the tournament director to write an article informing your golfers. In the process you will:

- establish another contact person between the tournament organizer and the golf courses -- increasing loyalty
- demonstrate a willingness to promote their tournament
- give them another reason to stay with you when it's time to set up their next tournament
- encourage other tournament directors to choose your golf course because they know you promote tournaments who choose your golf course

As one golf course operator once said, if it wasn't for tournaments, our golf course could be bankrupt.

Tournaments account for a large portion of golf course revenue. How many golf courses are promoting their tournaments to their audience? Not many.

In business, it's not what you know, it's who you know. Doing everything you can to help tournament organizers hold an event at your golf course will increase tournament play.

Call to Action

Call to actions are important in any marketing campaign. You can always use content to encourage your customers to do things, like sign up for your newsletter, like you on Facebook, buy your products, sign up for tee times, throw a party, buy some beer, or whatever else you want them to do.

As a rule of thumb, 90% of your posts should be to build a community by promoting engagement and interaction among your members. Less than 10% should of your posts should be used to sell or ask your members to do things.

Many golf courses make the mistake of spending 100% of their posts asking for sales.

Contests

At the golf courses we manage we always run a contest during the major championships and give golfers an opportunity to choose the pro golfers they think will shoot the lowest scores prior to the tournament. The winners received two greens fees at the course.

Other contest ideas would be:

- the first to comment on a post
- the best customer-submitted photograph
- the best customer-submitted video
- to guess what hole of a mysterious picture of your course
- to choose the best caption to a photo
- the first to answer a question correctly

Contests not only give your followers an opportunity to interact with your golf course, but they create word-of-mouth buzz. People continually talk about contests we've held online and in the real world. The engagement for our contest posts are exponentially larger than our regular posting.

Say thank you to all of your followers and fans by rewarding them. After all, if you're doing social media right, your followers are the ones helping to spread word of mouth for your golf course.

Discounts

Take back your golf course rates from the tee time wholesalers. Offer discounts on your terms. Reward Facebook followers for connecting with you. Give them an incentive to play your course at the times you want them to.

By offering your own discounts, you can make your golfers loyal to you. Have them sign up for your email newsletter list, "like" you on Facebook, and share their golfing experience with their family and friends.

Special Offers

Offer a free bucket of balls to people who check in. Give 10% off to those who take a picture at your course and share it on Instagram. Special offers like these create excitement, help build a loyal fan base and increase word of mouth.

Other ideas for special offers are:

- buy one, get one free
- golf lessons
- ball markers or golf balls

- sodas, cookies or chips
- a bucket of balls
- a round of golf

Golf Course Departments

In becoming a social golf course, every member of your staff should have a role. Whether your employees work in the pro shop, cart barn, food and beverage, maintenance or office staff, they can all participate in your social media campaign. We'll offer our blueprint for how you can get your staff involved in the next chapter.

Customer service is important. By assisting customers online and offline you can build a better golf course -- a social golf course.

Micro Content

For every piece of macro content you generate, you will have already created numerous opportunities for micro content. Micro content is smaller pieces designed to build engagement on sites like Facebook, Twitter, Instagram and others.

When posting micro content to Facebook, try to vary posts between text, images, and links.

Here are some forms of micro content you can use to get your golfers more engaged.

Statements/News/Updates:

Statements, news and updates inform your golf-ers. They help build involvement because they are re-al-time updates about the course. The most important component to these types of updates are the immediacy of the content posted.

Examples:

Text:

> *"Congratulations to O'Neills and Chef Platt for being named the Best Bar and Grill by Southland Golf Magazine! That is a lot of competition from LA to San Diego!"*

Image:

> *"Congratulations to lotrgolfer48 (Matt) in becoming GK's first two time GK Cup Champion! It was a great match vs. thingstodo."*

Quotes

Post quotes from famous golfers, professional golfers, or maybe even quotes you hear around your clubhouse, on the golf course, or in the pro shop. Give people an opportunity to share their thoughts on the quote. You can use serious quotes, or be more silly depending on your audience and what will appeal to them.

Examples:

Text:

"You might as well praise a man for not robbing a bank as to praise him for playing by the rules.' — Bobby Jones"

Image:

"It boils down to word of mouth. That's what drives most business.' - John Hakim"

Fill in the Blank

Fill in the blank responses should be simple and have short answers. The shorter the response, the more likely people will respond. For example, "The meaning of life is _____ will get less responses than, "The one word I'd use to describe the meaning of life is _____."

Examples:

Text:

"My favorite golfer is _____."

Image:

"The hole I enjoy most is _____."

Links

Links to your website or links to other websites that contain valuable information are great to use from time to time on your Facebook page. Make sure the goal of your links is to educate, inform or entertain. Be sure the content is valuable to your followers.

Facebook automatically populates links when you copy and paste them. Meaning when you type in the url of any website, Facebook will create the link for you. You can then delete the url and type in a reason for including the link, or ask a question based off of the information contained in the link you've provided.

For example:

Try typing the following link where you edit your Facebook page status: **http://socialgolfcourse.com** (and press space)

Facebook will automatically populate its page with a link to our website. Erase the link and include compelling text to encourage your followers to engage with the post or click on the link to find out more:

> *"Reading The Social Golf Course. A great resource for any golf course looking to increase rounds using social media."*

Questions

Questions encourage engagement. Questions should be to the point to get more interaction on your page.

Examples:

Text:

> *"How many rounds of golf do you plan on playing in 2014?"*

Image:

"What is the best driving hole you've ever played?"

Photos

Photos typically get a bigger response than written posts. Facebook is a visual platform and including pictures is a smart way to increase interest.

Another type of micro content you can use when posting a picture is having your followers create a clever caption for your Facebook posts. Try offering some sort of prize to the user who creates the most clever caption for the photo.

For example:

"Caption this."

* Easter Egg - To promote engagement, we've included this Easter Egg. If you're a golf course owner or operator, caption the photo below by sending an email with your caption to Zeb@WelbornMedia.com. Be sure to write Easter Egg in the subject line of your email so you'll be entered. The best caption as selected by the 19th Hole Media team will receive one free month of 19th Hole Media Facebook management - a $600 value. The winner will be chosen at the end of September, 2014 to be redeemed whenever convenient for the winning golf course. *

Testimonials

One of my favorite things to post is a testimonial from someone who said something nice about the golf course. Testimonials can come from a variety of resources . . . sometimes it comes from your Facebook followers, your Twitter followers, Yelp users or Greenskeeper.org users. Learn more about how to capitalize on people who say great things about your course in our chapter on Reputation Management.

For example:

"I am a regular player at Arroyo. The greens were brought all the way back 8 or so months ago and regularly roll around 10. First cuts are now in play and usually soft enough to force you to land your approach shots on the green. New greens keeper is awesome, totally improved the whole track.'

Thanks Brad Beer for the comment. Any other Arroyo Trabuco golfers want to chime in?"

Promotions

Giving away things is a surefire way to increase engagement on your social media platforms and word of mouth.

Many golf course operators are opposed to offering giveaways because it's difficult to measure the return on investment. Instead of thinking of what you can get from your promotions, think of using it as a way to say thank you. Every person who likes your Facebook page is giving you permission to send your marketing messages directly to them daily. This is valuable.

When you use promotions to say thank you, you are building rapport.

For example:

> *"The next 10 people to check-in at the golf course will receive a complimentary bucket of balls."*

Shout-Outs

I love giving shout-outs on my Facebook page to say how much we appreciate the efforts of someone on our staff, our customers, or people we come across in our community. Give recognition to people who are promoting your golf course.

For example:

"Photo by Twitter follower Michael Gonzalez - @ mgonz517. Thanks for playing Arroyo Trabuco Golf Club!"

Videos

YouTube videos can be used for macro or micro content. Vine and Instagram are other video applications that offer shorter video clips. Videos can help connect people to your golf course. You can see some videos we've done by visiting the 19th Hole Media YouTube page - http://bit.ly/19thplaylist

Events

Do you have events going on at your golf course? Why not publicize them regularly on your Facebook page. Promote events to help increase word of mouth.

For example:

"Do you have plans for Valentine's Day?"

Content Creation Summary

Your content needs to be interesting to the people who visit your golf course. If it makes them smile, laugh, click the like button, comment, share or triggers an emotional reaction then your content creation efforts are working.

Build a stronger connection with your golfers by creating compelling content. They will repay you by visiting you more often and playing more golf.

Discuss at SocialGolfCourse.com

What is your favorite 19th hole story?

CHAPTER 12

Implementing Social Media: Getting Your Staff Involved

To transform your golf course into a social golf course, it's important to have several members of your staff contributing. Your social media strategy is not just a media strategy, it's a people strategy.

With an organized effort and proper understanding, social media can be implemented at your golf course. Each platform can be used effectively by having different staff members responsible for updates and interactions.

The following is a list of tasks you can delegate to specific staff members. The more responsible staff members you can include the better.

Marketing

The marketing department should be the managers of social media at the course. It's important to understand how to market appropriately on the various social media platforms. If your marketing staff is not social media savvy, a social media agency -- like 19th Hole Media -- can manage or consult.

The marketing department should be responsible for:

- monitoring posts made on the golf course's social media channels
- searching the internet for posts made about the golf course
- directing social media discussions to appropriate staff members
- advising staff member(s) on the best ways to engage

It is important to know what is being said about your golf course on the internet and guide the discussion to make your golf course look good. There are many ways to find out what people are saying about your golf course on the internet:

- Google and YouTube - Conduct searches using your golf course name in the search bar
- Google Alerts and Tweet Beep - Visiting www.google.com/alerts or http://tweetbeep.com can help you create email alerts whenever a website or tweet mentions your golf course.
- Facebook - Monitor your Facebook page as users are allowed to leave reviews, add comments to your posts and send posts directly to your Facebook business page.
- Instagram, Pinterest, Twitter and Vine - Type in your golf course name in the search bar to bring up every post mentioning your course by name.
- Greenskeeper.org - Use the search feature to look for conversations about your golf course.

- Yelp & Tripadvisor - Search for your golf course to find reviews on your course.

The best way to respond to comments you find on the internet is to keep your tone of engagement authentic, professional and appreciative. If an internet user includes a comment or question which can be better answered by another member of your staff, bring them into the conversation. Critical reviews should be responded to quickly and politely (more later).

Top Level Management

Top level management should be involved in the general mission and direction of the marketing efforts of the golf course.

Golfers want to buy-in to the vision of a golf course. If top-level management can articulate the vision of the golf course, golfers and golf course staff will feel more connected.

The top-level manager is the glue that holds the course culture together. This person should work with the marketing department regularly to develop an understanding of social media to transition the golf course into a social golf course.

Social media should be discussed regularly in staff meetings.

In addition, top-level managers could thank customers in person and on social media. When a customer is thanked "from the top" it has a powerful impact. After interacting, conversations are likely to follow. A top-level manager can direct conversations to the staff members best qualified to engage the topic or issue.

When it comes to problem-solving and managing the reputation of the golf course, top-level managers should guide the response. When alerted of an issue, they should quickly and tactfully address it.

Turf Management

Turf management staff should have two roles on social media: to inform golfers of course conditions and educate golfers on turf maintenance.

They should keep the marketing, top-level management and other department heads informed on course conditions, current and future maintenance projects. And deal with any course-related social posts.

On Greenskeeper.org, turf management discussions are important. Many avid golfers appreciate the efforts taken to create a better golf course. If you're not articulating that to your customers, you're missing out on an opportunity for word-of-mouth marketing.

While working at Los Serranos Country Club, Superintendent Jose Prieto showed Zeb around the course pointing out maintenance projects. It was fascinating to see how much work was going into course improvements. Every time he visits Los Serranos, he still points out the improvements to the lakes on hole #7 on the South Course and hole #17 on the North Course to his playing partners. The discussion in our foursome when reaching those holes is about the golf course and the amazing job they did.

On the flip side, your golf course will not always be perfect, but it's important to point out problem areas so golfers know you are working to fix them. If they think you're not doing anything to solve the problem, your reputation could be tarnished.

Pro Shop Staff

Pro shop staff are perhaps the most direct contact point between a golf course and its customers.

Golf instructors can use social media to demonstrate expertise. As Frank Oppenheimer once said, "the best way to learn is to teach."

In providing golf tips, discussing proper etiquette and explaining rules -- through social media -- golf instructors can increase their knowledge while connecting with golfers through the computer and/or mobile phone.

Do you have an instructor who wants to give more lessons?

Post opportunities for free lessons to market your golf professional and get them the experience they need to attract more students. Golf instructors can take advantage of social media to create a higher demand for their services.

Beginning golfers could gain the confidence to reduce the intimidation many feel on the first tee. Newer golfers could develop a better understanding of the game before stepping foot on your golf course. Having your golf pro demonstrate expertise also encourages loyalty.

Golf instructors can also act as your front lines in the social perception of your course. In listening to the needs and desires of your golfers, golf instructors can provide valuable information you can use to enhance your social strategy.

Any great golfing stories or interactions with golf instructors should be sent to your social media outlets and shared with others.

Another opportunity for social media posts can occur during golf clinics and group instruction. Golfers, of all ages, are already in a social atmosphere while learning the game. Ask for permission from participants and/or guardians to snap some photos and/or videos for social media posts.

Invite participants to make social media posts and reference your golf course. Imagine how beneficial it would be to your junior golf programs if your participants consistently made posts of the fun they were having.

If an event, sale, tournament is taking place at your golf course, the pro shop staff should use social media to market those events -- in real-time.

Tournament/Group Staff

In our chapter on content creation, we discussed the benefits of promoting tournaments through your content. The tournament staff should be a bull horn -- on social media -- for your golf tournaments.

Tournament staff should be in charge of communicating with outside tournament organizers to make them aware of opportunities to connect with your golfers via social media, prior, during and after the event. Organizers can be given the option to promote their tournament through your email list, website, blog and Facebook page.

Wedding/Banquet Staff

Banquet staff have an opportunity to expose golfers and visitors to their banquet facilities. Pictures of events, testimonials and notification of events can develop leads for your banquet services.

For each event held at your golf course, banquet staff should use social media to:

• announce the event

- share pictures of the event
- congratulate and thank customers

If you want to secure more events for your facility, be sure to share photos and stories of successful weddings and banquets with your email list, blog, and social media followers.

Membership Staff

Golf courses that rely on memberships should have immediate success using social media. We'd argue that members often sign up for a membership at a golf course because they already know a member.

Membership staff should be in charge of communicating regularly with their clientele. By sharing photos, stories and videos of members through social media, you give them an opportunity to promote your golf course to their family and friends. Encourage them to share your posts and see your membership numbers rise.

Outside Services Staff

Beverage carts, snack stand personnel, cart attendants, starters, marshals and caddies can play a role in your social media campaign. They can report on social activity at your golf course and be asked to take pictures and/or encourage golfers to connect with your social media platforms.

Your outside services staff should be trained on how to encourage golfers to connect using social media. At many golf courses, cart attendants are the last ones to see your golfers. Have them hand out a flyer or business card encouraging golfers to like your golf course on

Facebook or sign up for your newsletter. This will help spread the word that you are a social golf course.

Snack stand, beverage cart personnel, starters and marshalls have a unique opportunity to connect with golfers out on the course. Have them take pictures of golfers to post on social media. Show everyone you have happy golfers and start developing ways to use word-of-mouth marketing to promote your golf course.

Caddies can demonstrate their expertise and share their course knowledge with your golfers. Not only will potential golfers get a better understanding of your course, but your caddies can demonstrate why golfers need them on the bag. They can also be a great source of information about your golfers.

For example, a caddie who witnesses a golfer record an eagle, a hole in one, or some other remarkable golf feat, can document the event with a picture/video and your golf course can share that information with your online community.

Food & Beverage

Entice golfers and local customers into the bar by sharing announcements, drink specials, and special events. Highlight some cool new draft beers, wines or appetizers and encourage more golfers to stop at the 19th Hole. Make golfers feel like your course is a great place to unwind after a round.

Implement an Effective Social Media Campaign and Educate Your Staff

Creating an organized social media campaign at your golf course is the key to success.

The first step to creating a campaign is to develop a consistent posting schedule. Delegate social activity to various members of your staff and hold them accountable. Stay on schedule. Having an infrequently updated social media presence can deter golfers from connecting with you.

The biggest advantage of social media is its ability provide real-time feedback. When a social media user engages with a post, respond quickly to extend the conversation.

Making a post and not responding to the feedback is the equivalent to hitting a green in regulation and then picking up your ball. Make sure you follow through or those commenting may feel as if you don't care about their opinions.

Notify patrons in person -- through signage and verbally -- about the social media platforms the golf course uses.

When having multiple people posting on your social media accounts, one thing to consider is identifying the author of the posts.

For example:

> *"Congratulations to our head professional for making the cut at the Farmer's Insurance Open at Torrey Pines this weekend. We're extremely proud. - Zeb - General Manager"*

By indicating the person who wrote the post, you are humanizing the experience. People are more willing to connect with other people more than they are willing to connect with a business. It's a great way to increase loyalty between your social media followers and your golf course.

Discuss on SocialGolfCourse.com

What other ideas do you have to get golf course staff more involved in the social media presence at your golf course?

CHAPTER 13

Managing Your Reputation

"More and more people are beginning to discover that there is no better way of spending a holiday, no more reasonable or less elaborate method of enjoying a day's outin, than playing good golf on good links." — Arthur Balfour[34]

The days of managing the perception of your golf course through ads in mass media channels like billboards, magazines, radio/televisions are gone. Consumers understand the difference between advertisements and original, customer-driven messages.

Most pictures used in a magazine ad and every radio and television commercial were carefully-crafted, professionally produced and seemingly picture-perfect. But today, customers naturally filter sales messages because the internet, search engines and social media provide a more accurate representation of your golf course.

---

34 Lewis, Peter N. The Dawn of Professional Golf: The Genesis of the European Tour, 1894-1914. New Ridley: Hobbs & McEwan, 1995. Print.

Ignoring negative social media conversations about your golf course can damage your reputation and deter customers from playing.

But when leveraged, social media can help a golf course curate the discussion to develop a positive impression of your golf course. So it's critical to know how to monitor golf course reviews.

How to Handle Negative Reviews

As the owner/founder of Greenskeeper.org, a golf social network in existence for more than a decade with 40,000-plus reviews from 64,000-plus members (of which over 70% are avid golfers), John has read every type of review imaginable.

One of the first questions he's always asked from Greenskeeper.org golf course clients and staff is:

What should I do when there is a negative review or comment posted about my golf course?

John's answer is almost always the same: take the high road.

If a review or comment bothers you or gets you riled up, look at it from a position of customer service. When you are engaging someone online treat them as if you are talking with them publicly, face-to-face.

In most cases, golfers are trying to be of service to other golfers and the golf course by leaving genuine, authentic feedback. Be grateful. The worst thing that can happen for a golf course is to have unhappy customers leave, say bad things about your course and never return. Now, you have a chance to address the golfer publicly and demonstrate you care about the experience golfers have at your course.

Every post is an opportunity to show others how much you respect and appreciate your customers. It's easy to think a negative review will damage your reputation, but responding to the review -- and how you respond -- is more important.

Ignoring or deleting negative comments is not the ideal customer service tactic.

Most golfers don't just read one review and form an opinion, they read multiple reviews to get a more complete perspective.

Once you start publicly engaging, involved readers will want their concerns addressed. A good way to begin is by expressing gratitude for the comment, and a desire to understand the concern. Try to defuse as much of the negative energy and shift it to a civil conversation. You're showing hundreds, maybe thousands of golfers, how your golf course treats customers.

In some cases, it might be wise to shift the conversation offline. Thank the golfer for providing feedback and ask them to contact you via telephone or email. Getting in a sparring match on social media will not be the best for your reputation.

Your responses to negative reviews should be handled on a case by case basis. Understanding the situation and working to solve the problem is the best customer service strategy. You should consider the possibility that when you publicly give away freebies, others may see an opportunity to leave negative reviews just to get free stuff.

In 2012, a good friend of Zeb's, Mike, recently retired from his job and was playing different golf courses to decide where he wanted to become a member. While playing at his favorite course, where he had played hundreds of times, his car was broken into. The staff at the course offered him free green fees, but did nothing to assist in repairing his vehicle. Mike took to social media to express his concerns, which were immediately deleted by the golf course.

Before his round of golf that day, Mike was most likely going to become a member and play golf regularly for years. Social media gave this golf course the opportunity to rectify a situation which could have provided them with thousands of dollars in revenue from a regular golfer and his playing partners. Shelling out the $300 or so it would cost to fix the problem could have created thousands of dollars in revenue for the course.

To this day, Mike plays up to 100 rounds of golf a year, but rarely at that golf course. He is upset about the experience he had there and still tells anyone who brings up the golf course about his horrible experience. Social media, through Mike alone (not to mention the additional golfers he would have brought to the golf course), could have made a substantial impact to the bottom line.

The social golf course would have known better.

Reviews on Greenskeeper.org

Greenskeeper.org has a community staff of 20-plus golfers that moderate reviews to ensure accuracy. If a golf course contacts Greenskeeper.org about a review, a member of the Greenskeeper.org staff will respond promptly. Other social media and golf course review sites do not have the same level of customer service.

Therefore, Greenskeeper.org is a great resource to evaluate how golfers perceive your course and take action to provide a better customer experience.

Here is an example from Greenskeeper.org of what can happen when a golf course takes the time to respond to a negative review:

robcanter

Posted: 06/08/13 10:32p

Member Since: Feb 24, 2005

From: Westwood, CA

> *"First let me say this is one of my favorite golf courses. I have been a member of the mens club the last two years but conditions have deteriorated. The course is in horrible shape and it was a crime to have to pay full price to play here. The greens are beyond slow. Not just aerated with large holes but lots of sand. The aprons were punched with large holes and have hardly healed. Putting and chipping are impossible.*
>
> *Fairways are very thin as is rough where there is any as there are mostly bare spots. Everything is a tight lie. Sand traps were hard and tee boxes uneven and beat up. Never seen it this bad. On top of that, it was over 5 hours to play. Two guys I played with have also played here for years and both said they are not coming back.*

No mention of any of this when we called for a reservation and when I went to the shop after, they agreed the course was in bad shape but did not offer any kind of refund or comp. It was basically, sorry and someone should have told you when you called.

Would stay away for at least a month and until you see several great reviews here."

After Golf Course Engaged:

robcanter

Posted: 06/10/13 9:22p

Member Since: Feb 24, 2005

From: Westwood, CA

Update on previous review:

> *"I got a call from Rodney at Rustic today.*
> *He wanted to discuss my review. He did take*
> *the time to explain their philosophy of course*
> *management and maintenance. In the end,*
> *we agreed to disagree on some issues. He had*
> *a fair point that the maintenance was listed*
> *on Greenskeeper.org which I did not check*
> *before going out. I am writing this because*
> *of how impressed I was that he picked up the*
> *phone to discuss the situation. It's nice to know*
> *that management really does care about the*
> *experience at the course. As I stated before, this*
> *is one of my favorite courses and I am sure given*
> *their commitment, the course will soon be back*
> *to the usual excellent conditions and I do look*
> *forward to going back."*

Great job Rustic Canyon Golf Course.

Focus on the Positive: Respond to Customers Who Say Great Things

Negative posts can light a fuse with most golf course operators and lure golf courses into spending most of their time addressing them.

But, it's the positive reviews and comments that provide golf courses with the best opportunities.

On Greenskeeper.org, the majority of reviews posted are positive. When a golf course is receiving positive reviews, it's course page on Greenskeeper.org gets 10 times as many page views compared to those that have neutral or negative posts.

When a golf course sees a positive post on Greenskeeper.org, Trip Advisor, Yelp, Facebook, Twitter, Google+ and others, they need to spring into action. Reply to it and note something specific about the post you appreciate and can start a conversation with.

On Greenskeeper.org, every golf course review has an e-mail icon next to the members name that can be clicked on to send a personal message expressing thanks. In addition, most golf course pages have a discussion section that can be used to reference a post and begin a conversation about it.

Always respond, but don't just say, "Thank you" because that is right where the conversation will end. Take action to promote the positive in marketing channels. For example, Greenskeeper.org integrates Facebook like boxes and tweets directly into its platform. Facebook allows golf courses to promote their page posts and embed posts on their own websites and within e-mails. Twitter allows promoted posts and embedding posts.

If a post is authentically positive and your golf course is having an engaging conversation bringing value to other golfers, by all means, promote and share it.

It's in your best interest to reward golfers who engage with you on social media. Rewarding golfers creates a valuable word of mouth opportunity. Personalizing your gifts depending on the conversation are an advanced social media tactic savvy marketers are integrating into their campaigns.

For example, if you're in a positive conversation regarding a golf course review, then give that person a discounted or free round of golf. If the conversation is about golf instruction, offer a discounted lesson. If it's about your food and beverage, a free drink is always nice. Whatever the context of the conversation is, connect your gift to it as much as possible.

You might be asking yourself how can I justify giving gifts away?

How can you afford not to?

Never underestimate the power of building relationships. Reinforcing positive word of mouth is one of the most important aspects of your marketing strategy. It's time to market like it's 2014 and not 2006.

To drive the point home, WestJet, a Canadian airline created a YouTube video titled, WestJet Christmas Miracle: real-time giving, in which they asked every passenger on a flight what they wanted for Christmas. By the time they arrived to their destination, every person on the plane got what they asked for. In giving, WestJet created a valuable word of mouth marketing opportunity for themselves. The video has been seen 35,333,104 times.

In thanking loyal customers, you create valuable word of mouth opportunities for your business. Prior to social media you could not benefit from word of mouth as rapidly as you can today. Run contests and give away goods to say thank you to your customers and substantially increase word-of-mouth marketing.

Be Proactive: Encourage Your Golfers to Leave Reviews

Concerning yourself with negative reviews means you're being reactive rather than proactive. Proactive businesses do better because they figure out ways to create a more memorable experience for their golfers. More golfers (as are people in general) are turning to review sites to make decisions about who they are going to do business with. The golf courses who have a proactive strategy to get golfers to review them positively will do better in the new economy.

As an owner or staff member of a golf course, one of your greatest responsibilities is providing valuable customer service. If you run a great business and are proud of the way you do things, asking for reviews should be a no-brainer. At the end of the round, ask your golfers to review your golf course on Greenskeeper.org, Facebook, Twitter, Yelp or any other review sites you see value in.

How Review Websites Can Make Your Business Better

Ultimately, review websites offer value for customers and businesses. Businesses have an opportunity to see mistakes they're making in their policies and correct them, resulting in happier customers. And customers have an opportunity to express their concerns about a golf course and their experience there.

At Greenskeeper.org, we received an email from a golf course superintendent in 2013, who said, "I found your site years ago, back when I worked under the very large (at that time) umbrella of (Name Removed Golf Management Company). Over the years I heard the public course strategy of not announcing aerifications and could never understand their thinking. I believe that your website put a stop to that and I applaud your efforts."

The golf course purposely failed to notify golfers of the course aeration schedule. Golfers would arrive at their course, pay full price and be upset when they found out the course was being aerated.

How much credibility do you think this golf course and golf management company lost?

Golfers, eager to share their unhappiness, actively searched for review sites like Greenskeeper.org to express their displeasure over the playing conditions and began playing courses who notified their golfers of the aeration schedule.

In the long run, the company in question reversed its policy. As a result of these reviews, they built a better experience for their customer which encouraged more golfers to play more often. Making happy customers will always be better than pissing them off.

On January 2, 2014 Zeb played golf at El Prado Golf Course in Chino, CA with his dad and a few friends. They had a great time. Zeb took a picture of his scorecard and posted the following caption to Facebook, Instagram and Twitter, "Two eagles and lipped out for a third. Final tally - 2 eagles, 2 birdies, 1 bogey and 4 doubles for a 75 at El Prado Golf Course."

On his personal Facebook page, he has 238 friends. His message about his round at El Prado Golf Course was sent out to all of them providing exposure for El Prado.

This golf course should have seen Zeb's post about his enjoyable experience at their course through Twitter and/or Instagram. A savvy marketer would have seen this post and shared it with their network. Currently, El Prado has 636 Facebook fans. Now, instead of reaching his 238 friends, this endorsement would have been seen by closer to 1,000 people.

Zeb's positive comment about his experience at El Prado Golf Course could have been seen by every person connected with El Prado via social media.

They could have shown their followers that fun, exciting things happen at their course. They could have built a stronger relationship with Zeb, someone willing to promote their course on his social media channels with more than 20,000 followers. They could have started a discussion helping to drive word-of-mouth marketing.

But, the opportunity was missed. And golf courses are missing opportunities like these every day.

Discuss on SocialGolfCourse.com

How do you handle positive or negative reviews at your golf course? Have any examples?

CHAPTER 14

The Social Golf Course

"If you watch a game, it's fun. If you play it, it's recreation. If you work at it, it's golf," — Bob Hope

Creating the social golf course will take work.

The best golfers in the world understand that hard work, commitment, dedication and talent achieve results.

As stewards of the game, it is our responsibility to grow it. We must give our golfers an opportunity to connect with one another, to play golf and to be social.

In 2014 and beyond let's agree to be caretakers of the game, to promote it and to innovate the game we love.

The social golf course is similar to the golf course I envisioned in the 1960s and 1970s with a bustling, vibrant and active clubhouse. Families gather on weekends, business transactions occur regularly and the community is fully integrated with the golf course.

Those who manage the social golf course will look for solutions to bring golfers together, to make the golfing experience more enjoyable and to connect golfers of all skill levels.

The best managers know that by building a social community at their golf course they are contributing to the longevity of the game, providing for a richer experience and building a better business.

Done well, good things will begin to take shape, including:

- Tee-time wholesalers disappearing
- Using online tools to develop a loyal customer base through newsletter signups, Facebook "likes," Twitter followers, and GK'ers.
- Offering discounts on their own terms, setting their prices and creating a loyal customer base.

Connecting golfers at their golf course -- online and off -- will be a priority. They will encourage social interaction and will share exciting golf experiences with their social media followers.

Messages will not be used as a direct sales push. Instead, they will focus on educating, entertaining and inspiring. They will create an active, engaged and loyal community of golfers.

The real value of social media lies with connecting golfers and retrieving feedback. Instead of guessing what customers want, social media gives an opportunity to address their concerns directly.

Done well, the business of golf will take care of itself.

The social golf course will constantly be looking to engage golfers on every social media platform, especially Facebook, Twitter and Greenskeeper.org. Finding local golfers online and reaching them effectively is the trick to developing a killer social media strategy.

Golfers want to engage with people, not brand names. Members of the golf course staff will participate in the social strategy, identify themselves and create their online personality in the process.

And, they will have a social media agency -- like 19th Hole Media -- to coach and assist them along the way.

The best golfers use coaches to improve their game. Most winning golf professionals will tell you that having a coach is essential.

Building a community of like-minded golfers to share their stories, triumphs and experiences at your golf course -- through social media word of mouth -- is how you become essential.

Content will be distributed daily through an email newsletter, a blog, social media outlets and in-person at the golf course.

Reputation management will be taken seriously. Monitoring what golfers say about you online -- through sites like Greenskeeper.org, Yelp, Google+, and Facebook -- and addressing their concerns quickly will create a loyal customer base.

The social golf course is proud of the product they produce. Every employee, from top to bottom, works to give the best golfing experience to every golfer that visits the course. And, the golf course will work to share that experience with as many people as possible.

Join us in improving the golfing experience through this fastest-growing, inexpensive and interactive way to reach golfers.

Use social media effectively and turn your golf course into . . .

The Social Golf Course.

Discuss at SocialGolfCourse.com

Do you have questions about how you can turn your golf course into a social golf course?

Connect With Us

Thank you for reading The Social Golf Course.

It's a work in progress. It reflects our love of the game and it captures our hopes to make it more social.

We encourage feedback, comments and thoughts. Consider this an invitation to all who want a healthier golf course industry. We value your opinions and ideas.

We will continue to revise The Social Golf Course on our website, SocialGolfCourse.com. Visit us and find up-to-date techniques, discussions and collaborative ideas.

We want to connect with you. Use the hashtag:

#SocialGolf

You can also find us at:

Zeb Welborn
Facebook: https://www.facebook.com/19thHoleMedia
Twitter: https://twitter.com/zebwelborn
LinkedIn: http://www.linkedin.com/in/zebwelborn
Email: Zeb@WelbornMedia.com
Phone: (909) 973 - 9089

John Hakim
Facebook: https://www.facebook.com/Greenskeeper.org
Twitter: https://twitter.com/JohnnyGK
LinkedIn: www.linkedin.com/pub/john-hakim/1/60/311
Email: golf@greenskeeper.org
Phone: (805) 807 - 5945

References

Portion of cover photo by Aberdeen Proving Ground photo (http://www.flickr.com/photos/usagapg/7166419024/) used under CC-BY (http://creativecommons.org/licenses/by/2.0/deed.en)/ Blurred from original and built upon

[1] Sounes, Howard. The Wicked Game: Arnold Palmer, Jack Nicklaus, Tiger Woods, and the Story of Modern Golf. New York: W. Morrow, 2004. Print.

[2] Cook, Kevin. Tommy's Honor: The Story of Old Tom Morris and Young Tom Morris, Golf's Founding Father and Son. New York: Gotham, 2007. Print.

[3] "Session 101: Opening Keynote - State of the Golf Industry." Proc. of Crittenden Golf Conference, Phoenix. N.p.: n.p., n.d. N. pag. Print.

[4] "According to Golf, the Economy Is Out of the Rough." Bloomberg.com. Bloomberg, n.d. Web. 12 Feb. 2014.

[5] "According to Golf, the Economy Is Out of the Rough." Bloomberg.com. Bloomberg, n.d. Web. 12 Feb. 2014.

[6] "Session 101: Opening Keynote - State of the Golf Industry." Proc. of Crittenden Golf Conference, Phoenix. N.p.: n.p., n.d. N. pag. Print.

[7] Hargreaves, Steve. "Why We're Working Less than Our Parents Did." CNNMoney. Cable News Network, 29 July 2013. Web. 12 Feb. 2014.

[8] "Session 101: Opening Keynote - State of the Golf Industry." Proc. of Crittenden Golf Conference, Phoenix. N.p.: n.p., n.d. N. pag. Print.

[9] "History of Golf - Scottish Perspective." History of Golf - Scottish Perspective. N.p., n.d. Web. 16 Nov. 2013.

[10] "History of Golf - Scottish Perspective." History of Golf - Scottish Perspective. N.p., n.d. Web. 16 Nov. 2013.

[11] Cook, Kevin. Tommy's Honor: The Story of Old Tom Morris and Young Tom Morris, Golf's Founding Father and Son. New York: Gotham, 2007. Print.

[12] "A Quick Nine: Best Golf Jokes." PGA.com. N.p., n.d. Web. 15 Feb. 2014.

[13] Wood, David. Around the World in 80 Rounds: Chasing a Golf Ball from Tierra Del Fuego to the Land of the Midnight Sun. New York: St. Martin's, 2008. Print.

[14] Shoemaker, Fred, and Pete Shoemaker. Extraordinary Golf: The Art of the Possible. New York: G.P. Putnam's Sons, 1996. Print.

[15] Shoemaker, Fred, and Pete Shoemaker. Extraordinary Golf: The Art of the Possible. New York: G.P. Putnam's Sons, 1996. Print.

[16] "Hitwise: Facebook.com Now Accounts For 1 In Every 5 Pageviews On The Web (In The U.S.)." TechCrunch. N.p., n.d. Web. 15 Feb. 2014.

[17] "Eric Schmidt: Every 2 Days We Create As Much Information As We Did Up To 2003." TechCrunch. N.p., n.d. Web. 19 Nov. 2013.

[18] "Google Plus Means SEO for Marketers." Search Engine Studio SearchEngineStudio.com. N.p., n.d. Web. 04 Jan. 2014.

[19] Cook, Kevin. Tommy's Honor: The Story of Old Tom Morris and Young Tom Morris, Golf's Founding Father and Son. New York: Gotham, 2007. Print.

[20] "Defining Success Podcast." Defining Success Podcast. N.p., n.d. Web. 15 Feb. 2014.

[21] "Session 101: Opening Keynote - State of the Golf Industry." Proc. of Crittenden Golf Conference, Phoenix.

[22] "Facebook." Wikipedia. Wikimedia Foundation, 16 Jan. 2014. Web. 16 Jan. 2014.

[23] "Facebook Statistics." Statistic Brain RSS. N.p., n.d. Web. 15 Dec. 2013.

[24] Outdoor Participation Report 2013. Rep. Outdoor Foundation, n.d. Web. 15 Feb. 2014.

[25] Canfield, Jack. Chicken Soup for the Golfer's Soul: The 2nd Round: More Stories of Insight, Inspiration and Laughter on the Links. Deerfield Beach, FL: Health Communications, 2002. Print.

[26] "Check-In Service Usage Has More Than Doubled In Past 9 Months, Study Says." Marketing Land. N.p., n.d. Web. 15 Feb. 2014.

[27] "Golf Entrepreneur." : Core Golfers & Technology. N.p., n.d. Web. 15 Feb. 2014.

[28] "Facebook Passes 1.19 Billion Monthly Active Users, 874 Million Mobile Users, and 728 Million Daily Users." TNW Network All Stories RSS. N.p., n.d. Web. 13 Jan. 2014.

[29] Welborn, Zeb. "Defining Success Podcast." Defining Success Podcast. N.p., n.d. Web. 15 Feb. 2014.

[30] Lednovich, Michael. "COURSES." COURSES. Southland Golf, n.d. Web. 15 Feb. 2014.

[31] Welborn, Zeb. "Defining Success Podcast." Defining Success Podcast. N.p., n.d. Web. 15 Feb. 2014.

[32] "Session 101: Opening Keynote - State of the Golf Industry." Proc. of Crittenden Golf Conference, Phoenix.

[33] Welborn, Zeb. "Defining Success Podcast." Defining Success Podcast. N.p., n.d. Web. 15 Feb. 2014.

[34] Lewis, Peter N. The Dawn of Professional Golf: The Genesis of the European Tour, 1894-1914. New Ridley: Hobbs & McEwan, 1995. Print.

Acknowledgments by Zeb Welborn

Thank you John Hakim for taking on this project with me. Your passion and enthusiasm for improving the golf experience is unmatched. I've enjoyed our long conversations about golf, social media and how to grow the game. I hope this is just the beginning.

Thank you to my Dad, Larry, and my Mom, Annie, for loving me unconditionally. And for being one heck of an editing team.

Thank you to my brother, Rocky, and my sister, Lacey, for being awesome.

Thank you to my wife, Cindy for showing me what love, commitment and devotion really means and for making daily sacrifices during this entire process.

Acknowledgments by John Hakim

Thank you Zeb Welborn for your unwavering dedication and love for the game of golf which is at the heart of this project. Together I believe our book has started a shift in the golf course industry to bring maximum enjoyment to golfers and ensure a healthy future for the game. Your expertise with social media combined with understanding of the golf course industry is truly impressive. It is a joy to be your friend and involved with this project.

Thank you to all the Greenskeeper.org members that inspire me everyday to live my dream being in service to others.

Made in the USA
Charleston, SC
03 June 2014